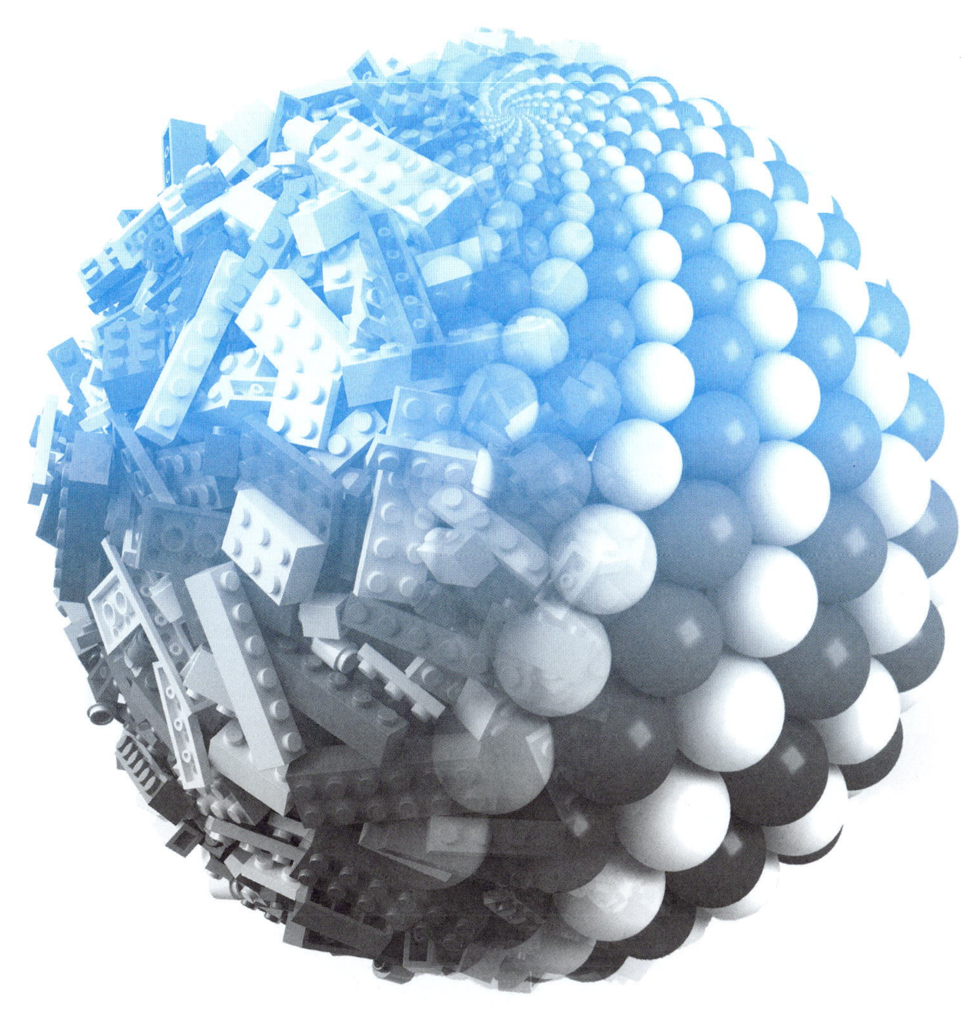

ALGEBRA 3/4

Walker Maths Essentials: Algebra 3/4
1st Edition
Charlotte Walker
Victoria Walker

Cover design: Cheryl Smith, Macarn Design
Text design: Cheryl Smith, Macarn Design
Production controller: Siew Han Ong

Any URLs contained in this publication were checked for currency during the production process. Note, however, that the publisher cannot vouch for the ongoing currency of URLs.

Acknowledgements
Cover photos courtesy of Shutterstock.

We wish to thank the Boards of Trustees of Darfield and Riccarton High Schools for allowing us to use materials and ideas developed while teaching. Our thanks also go to all past and present colleagues, especially Kath Wilson, who have generously shared their experience and ideas.

For product information and technology assistance,
in Australia call **1300 790 853**;
in New Zealand call **0800 449 725**

For permission to use material from this text or product, please email **aust.permissions@cengage.com**

National Library of New Zealand Cataloguing-in-Publication Data
A catalogue record for this book is available from the National Library of New Zealand

978 0 17044749 2

Cengage Learning Australia
Level 7, 80 Dorcas Street
South Melbourne, Victoria Australia 3205

Cengage Learning New Zealand
Unit 4B Rosedale Office Park
331 Rosedale Road, Albany, North Shore 0632, NZ

For learning solutions, visit **cengage.co.nz**

Printed in China by 1010 Printing International Limited.
2 3 4 5 6 7 25

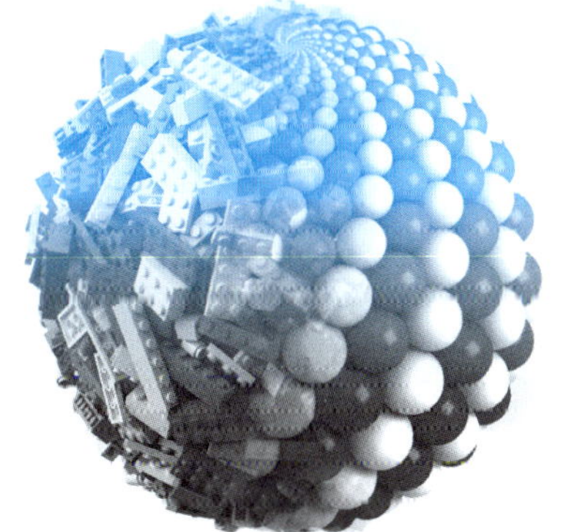

CONTENTS

Glossary **4**

Revision **6**
Working with integers 6

The language of algebra **10**
From words to expressions 10
Finding the value of a symbol 11
Phrases to expressions 13
More about variables 16

Simplifying expressions **17**
Multiplying 17
Dividing 19
Putting it together 21
Like terms 22
Adding and subtracting 23
Mixing it up 25
Challenge 1 26

Formulae and substitution **27**
With one variable 27
Challenge 2 31

Solving equations **32**
Adding and subtracting 32
Find the errors 36
Multiplying and dividing 37
Mixing it up 40
Challenge 3 41
Forming then solving equations 42

Understanding instructions in algebra **44**

Patterns **46**
Continuing patterns 47
From pictures to numbers 48
Describing patterns 49
Patterns into tables 51
Finding term 'zero' 54
Finding the rule from shapes and a table 57
Finding the rule from a description 64
Finding the rule from a list 68
Applications 70
Finding a term from a rule 72
Finding the sequence from the rule 74
Cross-number 77
Challenge 4 78

Graphs **79**
Plotting points 79
Positive coordinates 79
Zero coordinates 82
Putting it together 83
Plotting a pattern on a graph 84

Revision 1 .... **89**
Revision 2 .... **93**

Answers **97**

Glossary

Make your own glossary of key terms:

Term	Definition	Picture/Example
Expression		
Term		
Like terms		
Constant		
Power		
Index (plural: indices)		
Exponent		
Variable		
Coefficient		
Expand		

 ISBN: 9780170447492

Term	Definition	Picture/Example
Solve		
Simplify		
Substitute		
Evaluate		
Product		
Sum		
Numerator		
Denominator		
Sequence		
Origin		
Coordinates		

ISBN: 9780170447492

Revision

Working with integers

Multiplying and dividing integers

x/÷	+	–
+	+	–
–	–	+

Same signs ⇒ +
Different signs ⇒ –

Examples:
Different signs means –

–2 x +6 = –12

–6 ÷ +3 = –2

Same signs means +

+6 ÷ +3 = 2

–2 x –6 = 12

Remember, if there is **no sign**, it means **plus**.

If there is more than one multiply or divide sign, work from left to right.

–2 x –3 x –2 = (–2 x –3) x –2
= (6) x –2
= –12

Calculate the following.

1 3 x 6 = ________

2 5 x –2 = ________

3 –3 x –4 = ________

4 15 ÷ –3 = ________

5 –8 ÷ 2 = ________

6 –12 ÷ –4 = ________

7 –4 x 6 = ________

8 –10 ÷ –2 = ________

9 –3 x 2 x 2 = ________

10 –2 x 3 x –5 = ________

11 –16 ÷ –8 ÷ 2 = ________

12 –4 x –2 x –3 = ________

13 24 ÷ –2 ÷ 3 = ________

14 –2 x –3 x 5 x –1 = ________

ISBN: 9780170447492

Adding and subtracting integers

- Do this on the **number line**.
- On the number line, **start** at the position of the **first number**.
- Then move **left (–)** or **right (+)** as appropriate.

Examples:

1 –3 + 7 = 4

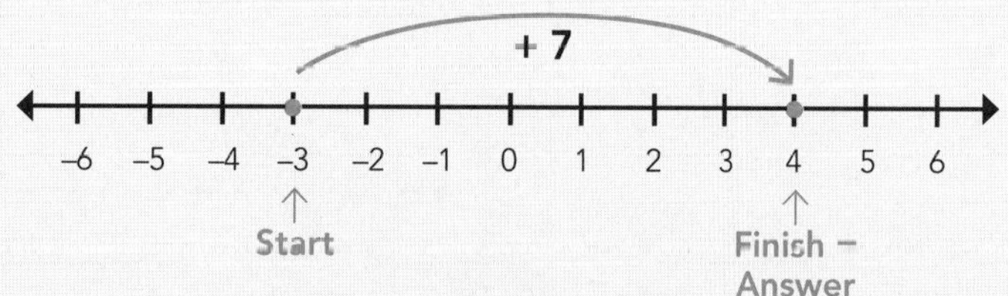

2 5 – 7 – 2 = –4

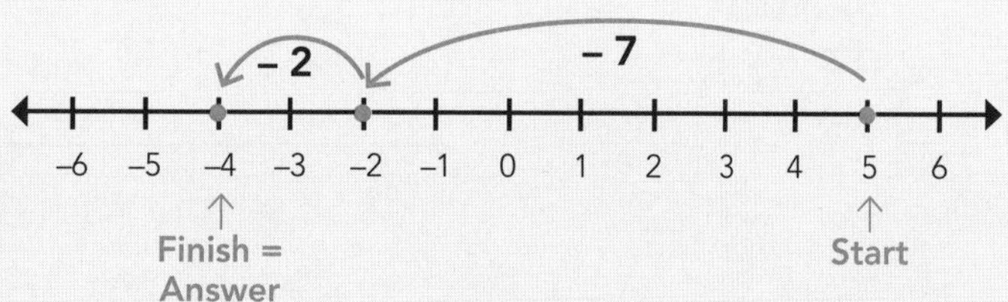

3 –4 + 9 – 3 = 2

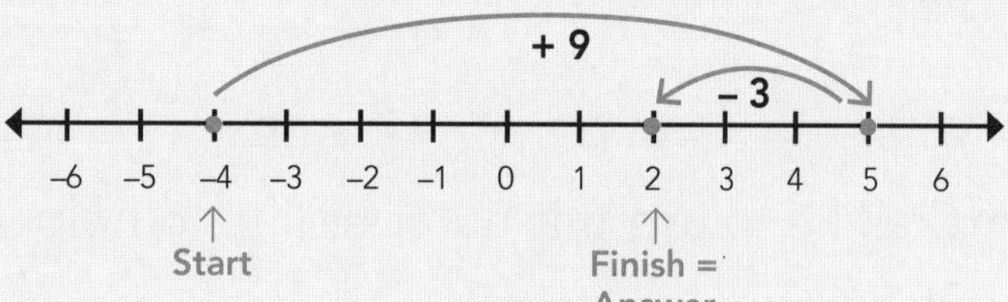

A short cut:

- You can **group** integers with the same sign.

4 **–4** + 9 **– 3** = 2
–7 + 9 = 2

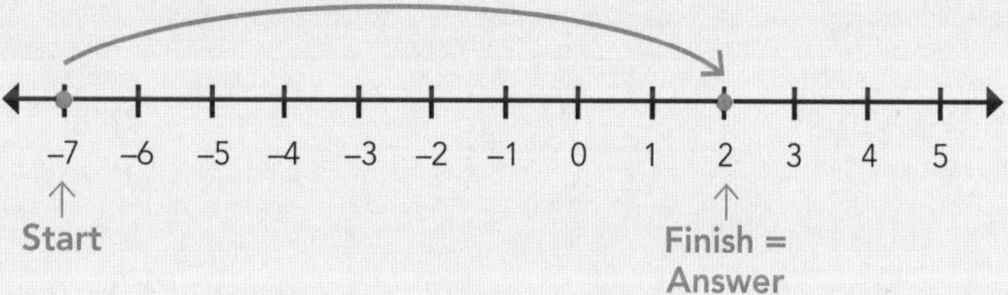

To help solve these questions, use the number lines and add arrows.

1 –3 + 7 =

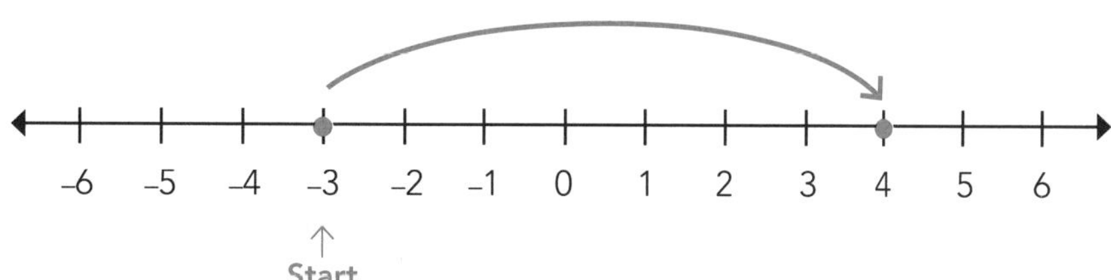

2 3 – 8 =

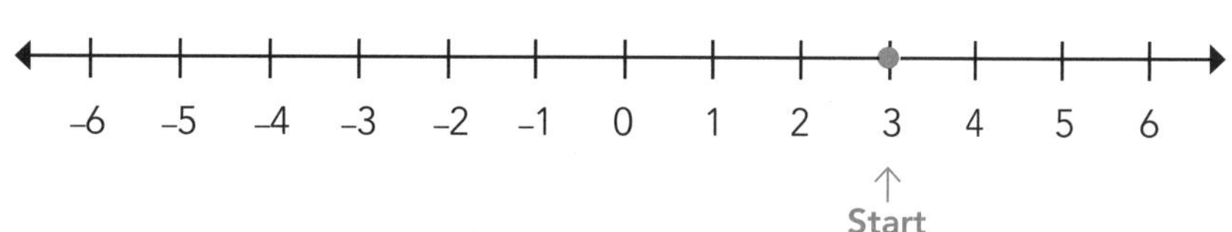

3 −3 − 2 = ______

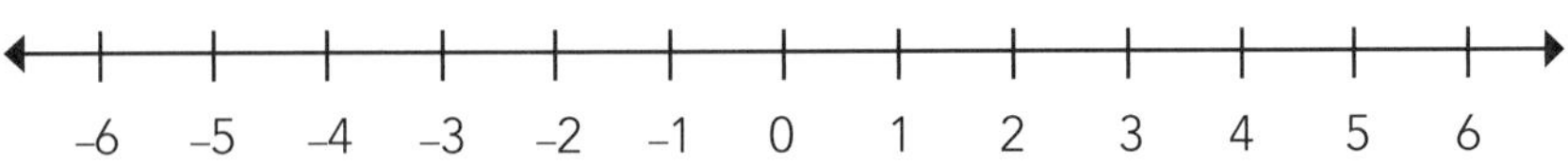

4 6 − 12 + 4 = ______

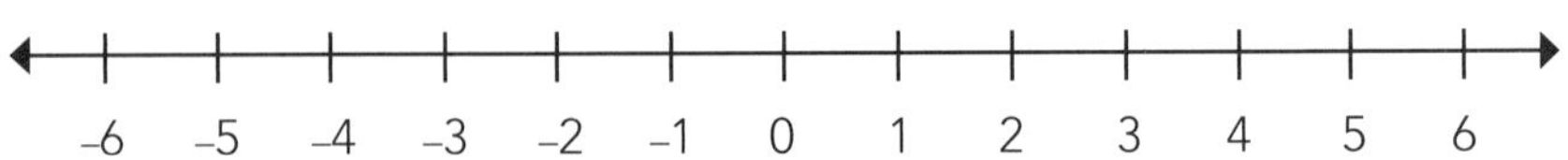

5 −4 + 5 + 3 = ______

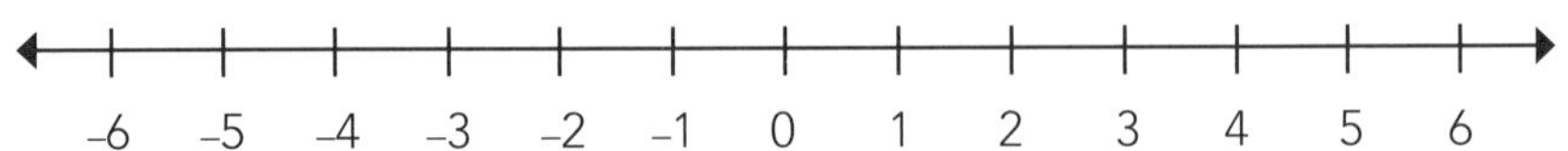

6 5 − 2 − 4 = ______

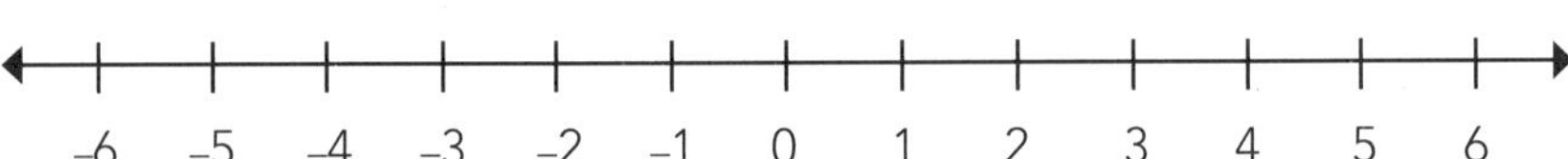

7 −3 − 1 + 4 + 2 = ______

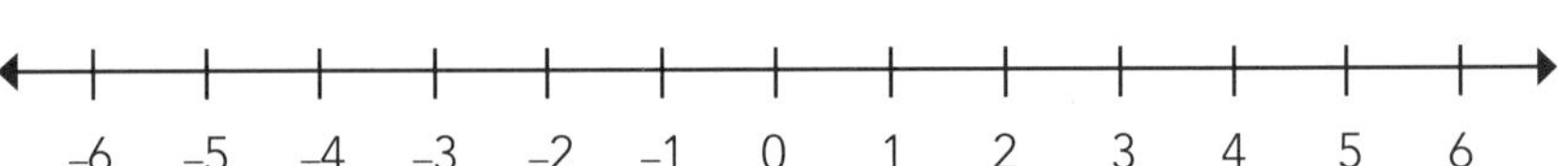

You make like to use this number line to help you with the following questions.

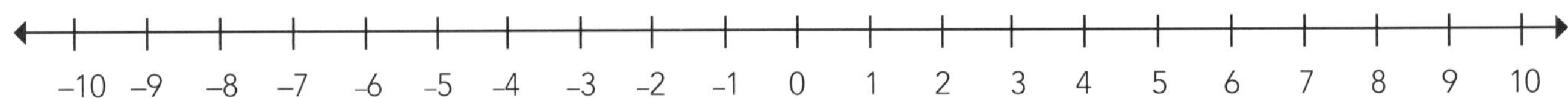

8 −5 + 6 = ____________

9 2 − 7 = ____________

10 −1 − 8 = ____________

11 −7 − 4 = ____________

12 −4 + 6 + 5 = ____________

13 2 − 8 + 3 = ____________

14 −2 + 9 − 3 = ____________

15 −7 − 3 + 8 = ____________

16 −10 + 5 + 3 = ____________

17 −6 + 9 − 2 = ____________

18 2 − 4 − 6 + 3 = ____________

19 −2 − 3 − 4 + 9 = ____________

ISBN: 9780170447492

Order of operations

- BEDMAS helps us to remember the order of operations.

Fill in the table below to help remember what order to complete calculations in:

B	
E	
D	
M	
A	
S	

Another word for these is **powers**, e.g. $2^3 = 8$.

Remember: when there is more than one of these, work from left to right.

Examples:

1 $12 - 3 \times 5$
$= 12 - (3 \times 5)$ — Multiplication first.
$= 12 - 15$ — Subtraction last.
$= -3$

2 $16 - (13 - 5) \div 2$ — Brackets first.
$= 16 - 8 \div 2$ — Division next.
$= 16 - 4$ — Subtraction last.
$= 12$

Use BEDMAS to calculate the following.

1 $2 + 4 \times 3 =$ ____________

2 $5 \times 2 - 9 =$ ____________

3 $12 \div 6 - 2 =$ ____________

4 $10 \times 6 \div 3 =$ ____________

5 $20 \div 4 - 2 =$ ____________

6 $10 - 4 \div 2 =$ ____________

7 $10 \times 6 \div 3 =$ ____________

8 $9 - 2 \times 3 =$ ____________

9 $24 \div 6 \div 2 =$ ____________

10 $10 + 6 \div 2 =$ ____________

11 $18 \div 3^2 =$ ____________

12 $12 - 4\,(1 + 2) =$ ____________

13 $2(7 - 3) =$ ____________

14 $2^3 + 5 \times 4 =$ ____________

ISBN: 9780170447492

The language of algebra

From words to expressions

Some **equivalent** expressions:

Written in words	Written using symbols
A number plus three	$p + 3$
Ten less than a number	$a - 10$
A number times six	$w \times 6$
A number divided by two	$c \div 2 = \frac{c}{2}$

Be careful to get these in the right order.

Write some other terms for these symbols. (Hint: use the list below if you are stuck.

1 + ______ ______

2 x ______ ______

3 – ______ ______

4 ÷ ______ ______

multiply, add, subtract, divide, minus, more, less than, plus, take away, times, goes into, lots of, division, sum, decrease by, total, split, product, increase by

Rewrite these as expressions using symbols. Use n as the variable.

5 A number plus five

= ***n*** ______ **5**

6 A number minus six

= ______

7 Three multiplied by a number

= ______

8 A number divided by eight

= ______

9 Seven take away a number

= ______

10 The sum of a number and twenty

= ______

11 The product of a number and two

= ______

12 A number decreased by ten

= ______

13 Four less than a number

= ______

14 Nine lots of a number

= ______

 ISBN: 9780170447492

Finding the value of a symbol

- The missing numbers in the following are represented by symbols:

2 + ★ = 7 — For this statement to be true, the symbol (★) must take the value **5**.

4 x ☯ = 12 — For this statement to be true, the symbol (☯) must take the value **3**.

8 + ☸ + ☸ = 12 — This time there are two symbols, so together they must equal 4 ∴ each symbol (☸) must take the value **2**.

Write down the value of each symbol for each of the following.

1 5 + ♣ = 7 ♣ = ______

2 10 – ✶ = 5 ✶ = ______

3 12 ÷ ♥ = 2 ♥ = ______

4 ☺ x 4 = 20 ☺ = ______

5 ⌘ + ⌘ + 3 = 11 ⌘ = ______

6 9 – ✠ – ✠ = 5 ✠ = ______

7 4 x ♠ + ♠ = 15 ♠ = ______

8 15 ÷ ⩓ – 3 = 2 ⩓ = ______

9 The value of each symbol is added to give the total in each row and column. Find the value of each symbol.

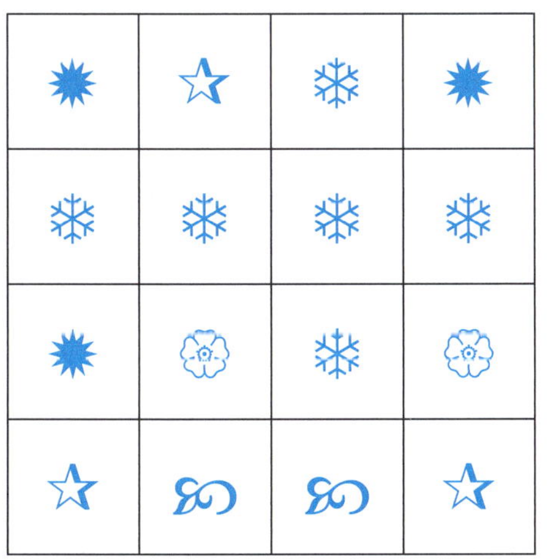

✹ = ______

☆ = ______

❄ = ______

✿ = ______

ဢ = ______

- In algebra, instead of using symbols like those on page 11, we use **letters**.
- The symbols used on page 11 can be replaced by letters.
- We call these letters 'variables' because they can take different values.

5 + ★ = 9:	$5 + s = 9$	**s** stands for **s**tar (★).
5 x ☯ = 10:	$5 \times y = 10$	**y** stands for **y**in-yang (☯).
12 – ☸ – ☸ = 4:	$12 - w - w = 4$	**w** stands for **w**heel (☸).

Write down the value of each variable (letter) for each of the following.

10 $3 + a = 8$ $a =$ ______

11 $12 - b = 3$ $b =$ ______

12 $20 \div c = 2$ $c =$ ______

13 $d \times 3 = 18$ $d =$ ______

14 $9 + e = 15$ $e =$ ______

15 $13 - f = 7$ $f =$ ______

16 $4 + f + f = 10$ $f =$ ______

17 $12 - g - g = 8$ $g =$ ______

18 $h \div 3 = 8$ $h =$ ______

19 $i \times 4 \times 2 = 40$ $i =$ ______

20 $2 + j + j + j = 23$ $j =$ ______

21 $k + k - 5 = 11$ $k =$ ______

22 $3(10 - m) = 18$ $m =$ ______

23 $6 + 12 \div n = 10$ $n =$ ______

24 $12 \div p - 2 = 4$ $p =$ ______

25 $q \times 2 - 4 = 18$ $q =$ ______

26 $r^2 + 4 = 20$ $r =$ ______

27 $14 - s \div 2 = 6$ $s =$ ______

28 $9(t - 2) = 27$ $t =$ ______

29 $u^2 - 10 = 15$ $u =$ ______

ISBN: 9780170447492

Phrases to expressions

- In algebra we use **operations** along with **variables** and numbers to write **expressions**.
- A **variable** is represented by a **letter of the alphabet**, which may be the initial of what it represents, e.g *d* for distance.

Some tricks:

- We do not write in the times sign between a number and a variable, e.g. 2*d* means 2 **x** *d*.
- We do not write an exponent for powers of one, e.g. d^1 is written as *d*.

Some special terms:

Double or twice *d*	$2 \times d$ or $2d$
Treble or triple *d*	$3 \times d$ or $3d$
Half of *d*	$d \div 2$ or $\frac{1}{2}d$ or $\frac{d}{2}$
Quarter of *d*	$d \div 4$ or $\frac{1}{4}d$ or $\frac{d}{4}$

Note that $2 \times d = d \times 2$, but we write the **number first**: 2*d*.

Remember that order doesn't matter when we add, so we can write $b + 10$ or $10 + b$.

Examples:

Phrase	Operation	Variable	Expression
10 more than *b*	+	*b*	$b + 10$ or $10 + b$
Five times *d*	x	*d*	$5d$
p reduced by 2	–	*p*	$p - 2$
a fifth of *m*	÷	*m*	$m \div 5$ or $\frac{m}{5}$ or $\frac{1}{5}m$

For division and subtraction order is important: $p - 2 \neq 2 - p$ and $m \div 5 \neq 5 \div m$

ISBN: 9780170447492

Match each phrase with the correct expression from the box below.

$e + 2$	$2e$	$\frac{e}{2}$	$e + 2$	$\frac{e}{f}$	$\frac{2}{f}$
$f - 2$	$2f$	ef	$\frac{f}{2}$	$f + 2$	$e - f$
$2 \div e$	$e - 2$	$f + e$	$2f$	$2 - f$	$e + f$

	Phrase	Expression
1	Twice *e*	
2	*e* reduced by two	
3	A total of *e* and *f*	
4	*e* shared between two	
5	Two more than *e*	
6	2 decreased by *f*	
7	Half of *f*	
8	*f* increased by two	
9	*f* subtracted from *e*	
10	*e* lots of *f*	
11	2 split between *e*	
12	The number of *f*s that go into *e*	
13	Two divided by *f*	
14	2 less than *f*	
15	Twice *f*	
16	*f* and *e*	
17	Double *f*	
18	The sum of *e* and 2	

ISBN: 9780170447492

Write an expression for each phrase. Use the variable *y*.

19 A term with two added to it

20 A variable multiplied by four

21 A variable divided by nine

22 Two with a number subtracted from it

23 Half a number

24 A number that is one less than a variable

25 Five less than a number

26 Ten divided by a number

Write a phrase for each expression.

27 $6 + a$

28 $7 - b$

29 $6c$

30 $d \div 2$

31 $e - 2$

32 $\frac{8}{f}$

33 $g \times 9$

34 $h + 3$

ISBN: 9780170447492

More about variables

- We use **letters** of the alphabet to represent **variables**.
- A **variable** is often a symbol for a value we don't know yet, and sometimes it is a quantity that **can change**.

Example:
Grandpa pays two of his grandsons to do a series of jobs during the school holidays, and pays them different amounts, depending on the job. They share the work and the money equally. They are paid:

\$15 for mowing the lawn:	Each grandson gets $\$\frac{15}{2} = \$7.50$
\$6 for cleaning the bathroom:	Each grandson gets $\$\frac{6}{2} = \$3$
\$10 vacuuming the floors:	Each grandson gets $\$\frac{10}{2} = \$5$

We call the total amount they were **paid** for each job ***p***, so each grandson was paid $\$\frac{p}{2}$ for each job.

$\frac{p}{2}$ is called an **expression**.

p is called the **variable** and it represents the amount that Grandpa **pays** for each job. *p* **changes** depending on how much is paid for each job.

Identify the variable and the expression.

1 Eddie was paid \$12 per hour for helping with the housework. He found that the total he was paid each day was given by the expression **Total = 12*h***.

a The variable is _____ and it stands for ______________________________.

b Use the expression to calculate how much he would be paid for four hours of housework.

Total = 12*h*
= 12 x ________
= \$ ________

2 Aroha is allowed a total of 10 at her birthday party (including herself). She has several cousins who might come, as well as some friends. The number of friends she can ask is given by the expression **Number of friends = 10 – *c* – 1**.

a The variable is _____ and it stands for ______________________________.

b If three cousins can come, use the expression to calculate how many friends she can ask.

Total friends = 10 – *c* – 1
= 10 – ________ – 1
= ________

ISBN: 9780170447492

Simplifying expressions

Multiplying

The order within simplified expressions should be:

sign	number	letters
Only if the term is **negative**.	We call this the '**coefficient**'.	We call these '**variables**' and they should appear in **alphabetical order**.

Examples:

Unsimplified expressions	Simplified expressions
$a \times 2$	$2a$
$a \times a \times a$	a^3
$5 \times a \times b$	$5ab$
$3a \times 2a$	$6a^2$
$2c \times -4b$	$-8bc$
$b \times c \times 2 \times a$	$2abc$

Index form or **power form**. (a^3, $6a^2$)

Circle/highlight the correct/best simplified answer for each of the following.

	Expression		
1	$5 \times a$	$a5$	$5a$
		5^a	a^5
2	$b \times b \times b$	b^3	3^b
		$3b$	$b3$
3	$c \times 3 \times d$	$cd3$	cd^3
		$3cd$	c^3d
4	$4e \times 2$	$e8$	$8e$
		$4e^2$	$2e^4$
5	$3f \times 2g$	f^3g^6	fg^6
		$6fg$	$6gf$
6	$4h \times 3h$	$12h$	$12h^2$
		$7h^2$	$4h^3$
7	$4 \times -j$	$4j$	$-4j$
		$j4$	$-j4$
8	$-k \times k$	$-2k$	k^2
		$2k$	$-k^2$

ISBN: 9780170447492

Simplify the following expressions.

9 $b \times 2 =$ __________

10 $c \times p =$ __________

11 $8 \times d =$ __________

12 $2 \times e \times b =$ __________

13 $f \times f =$ __________

14 $g \times s \times 4 =$ __________

15 $3 \times h \times h =$ __________

16 $-3 \times h \times g =$ __________

17 $2 \times n \times -4 =$ __________

18 $-5p \times -2 =$ __________

19 $-4m \times -6m =$ __________

20 $t \times n \times n =$ __________

21 $s \times s \times u \times u =$ __________

22 $-7v \times -v =$ __________

23 $-3p \times 6p \times p =$ __________

24 $q \times -2z \times q =$ __________

25 Join the dots to match each term on the left with the like term on the right.

$3 \times 2 \times t$ •	• $-6s$
$s \times -6 \times t$ •	• $-6s^2$
$2 \times s \times -3 \times s$ •	• $6s^2$
$t \times -6 \times 1 \times t$ •	• $-6t^2$
$-s \times 2 \times -3$ •	• $6t^2$
$-t \times -6 \times t$ •	• $6st$
$2 \times 3 \times s \times t$ •	• $-6st$
$2 \times t \times -3$ •	• $6t$
$1 \times s \times -6$ •	• $6s$
$2s \times -3 \times -s$ •	• $-6t$

ISBN: 9780170447492

Dividing

- 'x divided by y' can be written as either $x \div y$ or $\frac{x}{y}$.
- Don't forget that $\frac{x}{x} = 1$, so you can 'cancel'.

Example: $\frac{10b}{2} = \frac{5b}{1} \times \frac{2}{2}$

$= 5b$

Remember:

1 $\frac{\text{anything}}{1}$ = itself e.g. $\frac{2}{1} = 2$

2 $\frac{\text{anything}}{\text{itself}} = 1$ e.g. $\frac{2}{2} = 1$

More examples:

Unsimplified expressions	Simplified expressions
$a \div 3$	$\frac{a}{3}$ or $\frac{1}{3}a$
$2 \div a$	$\frac{2}{a}$
$\frac{3a}{6}$	$\frac{a}{2}$ or $\frac{1}{2}a$
$\frac{8b}{2a}$	$\frac{4b}{a}$

Circle/highlight the expression that is the *best* match for each of the following.

1 $b \div 4$

$4b$	$b4$
$\frac{b}{4}$	$\frac{4}{b}$

2 $5 \div p$

$\frac{p}{5}$	$\frac{5}{p}$
$5p$	$p5$

3 $8a \div 2$

$\frac{1}{4}a$	$\frac{1}{4a}$
$4a$	$a4$

4 $\frac{4}{12d}$

$\frac{1}{3d}$	$\frac{1}{3}d$
$d3$	$3d$

ISBN: 9780170447492

Simplify the following expressions.

5 $3y \div 6 =$ ______________

6 $14d \div 7 =$ ______________

7 $20 \div 2e =$ ______________

8 $12b \div 1 =$ ______________

9 $15b \div 15 =$ ______________

10 $\frac{5g}{15} =$ ______________

11 $\frac{4}{20p} =$ ______________

12 $\frac{21h}{7h} =$ ______________

13 $\frac{18m}{3} =$ ______________

14 $\frac{2}{16a} =$ ______________

15 $\frac{25a}{25a} =$ ______________

16 $\frac{8b}{b} =$ ______________

17 $24 \div 3v =$ ______________

18 $\frac{-6b}{2} =$ ______________

19 Join the dots to match each term on the left with the simplified term on the right.

$12f \div 6$ •	• $-\frac{f}{2}$
$\frac{-10}{5f}$ •	• $\frac{f}{2}$
$\frac{14}{7f}$ •	• $-\frac{2}{f}$
$8f \div 16$ •	• $-2f$
$\frac{20f}{-10}$ •	• $\frac{2}{f}$
$-9f \div 18$ •	• $2f$

ISBN: 9780170447492

Putting it together

Use the simplified terms in the boxes as answers to the questions below. You should use each answer only once.

d	$\frac{2}{d}$	2	$\frac{d}{2}$
$-6e$	d^2	$2e$	6
$2de$	1	$-d$	$2d$
$-e$	$6e$	$-6d$	$-2d$

Simplify each of the following.

1 $d \times 2 =$ ______________

2 $e \times 2 \times d =$ ______________

3 $\frac{6e}{3} =$ ______________

4 $2e \times 3 =$ ______________

5 $\frac{6}{3d} =$ ______________

6 $\frac{2d}{d} =$ ______________

7 $3e \div 3e =$ ______________

8 $\frac{2d}{4} =$ ______________

9 $6c \div c -$ ______________

10 $-3 \times d \times 2 =$ ______________

11 $\frac{3e}{-3} =$ ______________

12 $-2d \div 2 =$ ______________

13 $-\frac{6d}{3} =$ ______________

14 $d \times d =$ ______________

15 $\frac{2d}{2} =$ ______________

16 $2 \times -3e =$ ______________

ISBN: 9780170447492

Like terms

- Terms can only be added or subtracted if they are '**like terms**'.
- 'Like' terms must have exactly the **same variables**, and each variable must be raised to exactly the **same power**.
- Order does not matter.
- The sign does not matter.

Examples: The following **are** like terms: p, $-p$, $3p$ and $-5p$
qr, $2qr$, rq and $-qr$.

The following are **not** like terms:

a and 2 — Second term does not have an **a** term.

ab and ba**c** — Second term includes a '**c**' term.

ab^2 and ab — First term has b^2, but second term does not.

State whether each of the following pairs are like terms or unlike terms.

1 x and y ____________

2 x and $3x$ ____________

3 x and 3 ____________

4 2 and 3 ____________

5 $-x$ and $3x$ ____________

6 x and x^2 ____________

7 x and $100x$ ____________

8 $3y$ and $3x$ ____________

9 xy and yx ____________

10 $2xy$ and xy ____________

11 -2 and $-y$ ____________

12 $2x$ and x^2 ____________

13 xy and x^2y ____________

14 xy^2 and y^2x ____________

15 Circle the like terms.

$2p$, p^2, 2, $-p$, $10p$, q, p, pq

ISBN: 9780170447492

Adding and subtracting

- When adding or subtracting, you can **combine only like terms**.
- Only the ones with exactly the same variables and powers can be combined.

Hint: It is helpful to circle, underline or highlight terms that are 'like' each other with the same colour.

Examples: Simplify the following.

1 $3p + 2r + p = 4p + 2r$

$3p$ and $+p$ are like terms, so they can be combined $\Rightarrow 4p$.
$2r$ has no other like terms so remains the same.

2 $5a + 2b - a = 4a + 2b$

$5a$ and $-a$ are like terms, so they can be combined $\Rightarrow 4a$.

Remember, the sign before the term belongs to it.

A Fill the boxes with signs, letters and numbers in order to complete a correct simplification.

1 $a + a =$ ☐

2 $t + t + t + t =$ ☐

3 $4y + y =$ ☐

4 $7d - 2d =$ ☐

5 $5a + 3a =$ ☐

6 $6b + b - 2b =$ ☐

7 $2g + 1 + 4 = 2g +$ ☐

8 $a + b + 3a + 5b = 4a +$ ☐

9 $3f + 2p + p - f =$ ☐ $+ 3p$

10 $5y + 2 - y - 6 = 4y$ ☐

11 $7z + 9y - 2z - y = 5z +$ ☐

12 $6p + 2w - 2p + p =$ ☐ $+ 2w$

13 $3d + 4e - 5e - 2d = d$ ☐

14 $5b - 4c - b + 7c = 4b +$ ☐

ISBN: 9780170447492

B Circle/highlight the correct/best simplified answer for each of the following.

	Question				Question		
1	$p + p =$	p^2	$p2$	**2**	$3a + 6a =$	$18a$	$9a$
		$2p$	${}^2p$			a^{18}	a^9
3	$9a + 4$	$13a$	$9a + 4$	**4**	$3b + c + 5b$	$8b + c$	$8bc$
		13	$36a$			$3b + 6c$	$8b^2 + c$
5	$7a + a + a$	$7aaa$	$7a^3$	**6**	$f + f - f$	$3f$	$2f$
		$7a$	$9a$			$1f$	f
7	$5a - 2 + a$	$4a$	$6a + 2$	**8**	$6y - 2y + y$	$5y$	$4y$
		$6a - 2$	$3a$			$4yy$	$3y$
9	$3b - b$	3	$3b$	**10**	$a - b + 3a - 2b$	$3a - 4b$	$4a + 3b$
		$4b$	$2b$			$4a - 3b$	$3a + 4b$

C Simplify these by adding or subtracting like terms.

1 $a + a =$ ____________ **2** $x + 2x =$ ____________

3 $5a + a + 3a =$ ____________ **4** $2y + 3y - y + 4y =$ ____________

5 $7a + 2b + a =$ ____________ **6** $y + y + 6 =$ ____________

7 $2x + 4 - x =$ ____________ **8** $2a + 3b + a =$ ____________

9 $4x + 7y - x - 2y =$ ____________ **10** $3p + 6q - 2p - q =$ ____________

11 $7a - a + 5b + 4 =$ ____________ **12** $9y + 7 - x - 2 =$ ____________

13 $4f + 3g - f - 7g =$ ____________ **14** $x - 4y + 3x + y =$ ____________

ISBN: 9780170447492

Mixing it up

Some of the following simplifications are correct and some are incorrect. If the simplification is correct, put a tick in the ✓/✗ column. If it is incorrect, put a cross in the ✓/✗ column, and write the correct answer.

		✓/✗	Correct solution
1	$p \times p \times 2 = 2p$		
2	$\frac{12pq}{4} = 3pq$		
3	$a + a^2 + a = a^2 + 2a$		
4	$2t \times 5t = 10t$		
5	$6a + a - 2 - a + 7 - 6a + 9$		
6	$10m \div 2m = 5m$		
7	$15f + 2g - 10f - g = 5f - g$		
8	$-24 \div 8c = \frac{-3}{c}$		

ISBN: 9780170447492

Challenge 1

1 Highlight the boxes which contain an expression that is equivalent to the central expression.

$7a + b + 5a - b$	$\frac{24a}{2}$	$12 \times a \times a$	$10a - a + a$
$17a - 5a$			$3a \times 4$
	$12a$		
$\frac{2}{24a}$			$15a - 3$
$20a - 7a - a$	$12a \times 1$	$15a - 3a + 1$	$24a \div 2a$

2 Solve the following puzzles.

If:

x = 16

 x  x = 36

 x  x  = 72

Then:

 = ____________

= ____________

= ____________

 ISBN: 9780170447492

Formulae and substitution

With one variable

What is a formula? A formula is an **algebraic expression** of a **rule**.

Examples:

This is a square with sides L cm long:

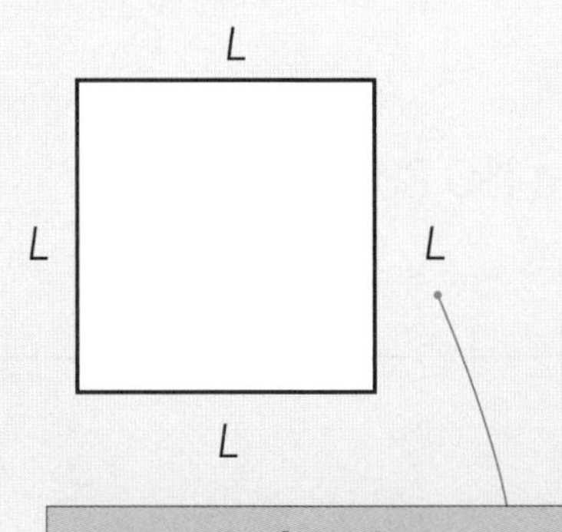

L stands for the **Length** of each side, so this is the **variable**.

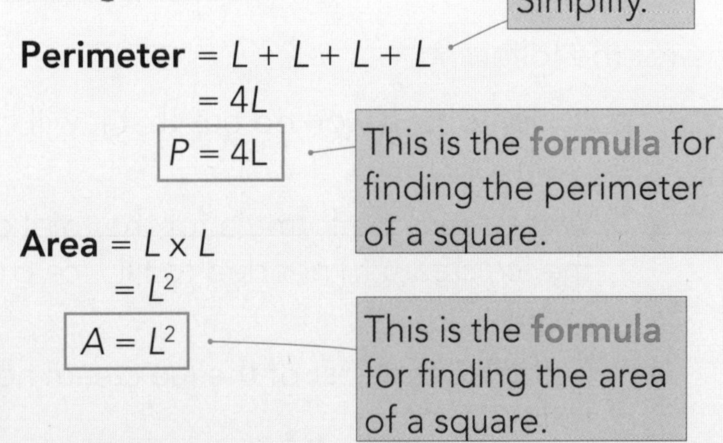

Perimeter $= L + L + L + L$

$= 4L$

$P = 4L$

Simplify.

This is the **formula** for finding the perimeter of a square.

Area $= L \times L$

$= L^2$

$A = L^2$

This is the **formula** for finding the area of a square.

What is substitution? Substitution is when you **replace variables with numbers**.

But don't forget **BEDMAS** when doing this.

Examples:

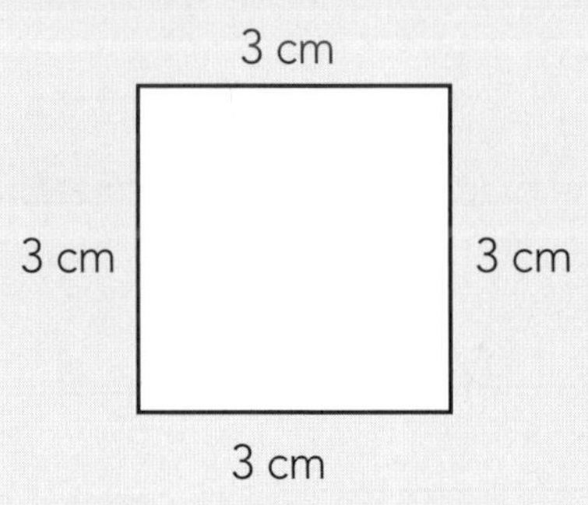

Perimeter $P = 4L$

$= 4 \times 3$

$= 12$ cm

For this square we know that $L = 3$, so we **substitute** L with **3**.

Area $A = L^2$

$= 3^2$

$= 9\ \text{cm}^2$

Don't forget the units.

Some more examples:

1 Trashy Taxis will charge the school \$10 plus \$3 per kilometre to take the tennis team to their game. The formula for the total fare is $C = 10 + 3k$, where k stands for the number of **kilometres**. Calculate the charge if their game is 9 km away.

$C = 10 + 3k$

$= 10 + 3 \times 9$

$= \$37$

Replace k by the number of **kilometres**.

ISBN: 9780170447492

2 The class is going to make and sell ice creams at the school fair. Each cone costs 30c. The formula for the total cost of cones (C) (in dollars) for making i ice creams is $\mathbf{C = 0.30}\boldsymbol{i}$. Calculate the total cost of the cones if they make 200 ice creams.

$$C = 0.30i$$
$$= 0.30 \times 200$$
$$= \$60.00$$

Notice that there should be just **one** '=' sign per line, and they are **lined up** under each other.

Answer the following.

1 The students have worked out that it will cost 80c ($0.80) to fill each cone with ice cream.

a Write down the formula for the total cost of the ice cream (I) needed to fill i ice cream cones: I = ______

b Calculate the cost of the ice cream needed to fill 200 cones: I = ______
= ______ x ______
= ______

c Complete the formula for finding the total cost (T) of 200 filled ice cream cones. $T = 0.30i$ + ______
= ______ i
= ______ x ______
= $ ______

d They sell each ice cream for $3. Write down the formula for the amount of money (M) that they get for selling i ice creams. M = ______

e How much money (M) did they get for selling 200 ice creams? M = ______
= $ ______

f Their profit (P) is the amount of money (M) that they got for selling the ice creams minus the total cost (T) of the cones and the ice cream. Calculate their profit if they sell 200 ice creams. $P = M$ – ______
= $ ______ – $ ______
= $ ______

ISBN: 9780170447492

2 Holly earns \$15 per hour picking fruit in her parents' orchard. The formula for the amount she gets paid is $A = 15h$, where h stands for the number of hours she has worked.

a How much would she get paid for working six hours?

A = ______________

= ________ x ________

= \$______________

b She also gets paid \$12 per hour for gardening for her aunt. Write a formula for the amount that she is paid for gardening.

A = ______________

c On Saturday morning she could pick fruit for three hours or garden for four hours. Which would earn her the most money? Show your calculations.

Fruit-picking earns ______________ Gardening earns ______________

= ______________ = ______________

______________________________ earns more money by \$______________.

d She also bikes to her grandmother's house and helps her with a variety of jobs. The formula for the amount her grandmother pays her is $A = 14h + 10$, where h stands for the number of hours she is there. Explain what this formula means in this context.

____

____

e When Holly babysits for her aunt, she is paid \$13 per hour, plus her return bus fare which is \$7. Write a formula for how much she is paid for babysitting.

A = ______________

3 Cut-rate Cabs will charge \$20 to take the tennis team to their game, plus \$2 per kilometre. Let k stand for the number of kilometres. (See Example 1 on page 27.)

a Write down the formula for calculating the total charge.

C = ______________

b Calculate the charge for taking the tennis team to the game which is 9 km away.

C = ______________

= ______________

= \$ ______________

ISBN: 9780170447492

4 Complete the following table.

Formula	$b = 1$	$b = 2$	$b = 5$	$b = 10$
$A = 3b$	$A = 3b$ $= 3 \times 1$ $= 3$	$A =$ ______ $=$ ______ $=$ ______	$A =$ ______ $=$ ______ $=$ ______	$A =$ ______ $=$ ______ $=$ ______
$A = b + 7$	$A =$ ______ $=$ ______ $=$ ______	$A =$ ______ $=$ ______ $=$ ______	$A =$ ______ $=$ ______ $=$ ______	$A =$ ______ $=$ ______ $=$ ______
$A = 20 - b$	$A =$ ______ $=$ ______ $=$ ______	$A =$ ______ $=$ ______ $=$ ______	$A =$ ______ $=$ ______ $=$ ______	$A =$ ______ $=$ ______ $=$ ______
$A = b - 4$	$A =$ ______ $=$ ______ $=$ ______	$A =$ ______ $=$ ______ $=$ ______	$A =$ ______ $=$ ______ $=$ ______	$A =$ ______ $=$ ______ $=$ ______
$A = \frac{20}{b}$	$A =$ ______ $=$ ______ $=$ ______	$A =$ ______ $=$ ______ $=$ ______	$A =$ ______ $=$ ______ $=$ ______	$A =$ ______ $=$ ______ $=$ ______
$A = b^2$	$A =$ ______ $=$ ______ $=$ ______	$A =$ ______ $=$ ______ $=$ ______	$A =$ ______ $=$ ______ $=$ ______	$A =$ ______ $=$ ______ $=$ ______
$A = 5 - 2b$	$A =$ ______ $=$ ______ $=$ ______	$A =$ ______ $=$ ______ $=$ ______	$A =$ ______ $=$ ______ $=$ ______	$A =$ ______ $=$ ______ $=$ ______

ISBN: 9780170447492

Challenge 2

Substitute with the following values in order to complete the cross-number:

$w = 12 \quad y = 2 \quad z = 6$

	1	2		3		
4						5
6			7		8	
		9				
10					11	12
		13		14		
	15			16		

Across		Down	
1	$2z$	**2**	$w \times y$
3	z^2	**3**	$2w + 10$
6	$\frac{66}{z}$	**4**	$33 - w$
8	$9z - 1$	**5**	$\frac{2w + y}{2}$
9	w^2	**7**	$2wz$
10	$5w + yz$	**10**	$wz - y$
11	$10z + 3w - 10$	**12**	$wy^2 + w$
15	$\frac{3w + 2}{y}$	**13**	$\frac{z^2}{2} + w - 1$
16	$3wy - 4$	**14**	$w \div y \times z$

Solving equations

- 'Solve' means **'find the value for x'**.

Rules:

1. You can do anything you like to an equation as long as you do the **same to both sides**.
2. There should be only **one equals sign** per line.
3. Collect all the variables on one side and numbers on the other side.
4. When you want to get rid of something, perform the **opposite** operation.
5. Your aim is to get **x =** ....

Adding and subtracting

Examples:

We need to get rid of the **– 5** from the left side.

1

$$x - 5 = 9$$

Do the **opposite** of **– 5. Add 5** to **both** sides.

$$x - 5 + 5 = 9 + 5$$

$$x = 14$$

This is our aim: to have the variable on the left and its value on the right.

Notice that there should be just **one** '=' sign per line, and they are **lined up** under each other.

We can always **check** that the solution works: $14 - 5 = 9$ ✓

We need to get rid of the **+ 7** from the left side.

2

$$t + 7 = 2$$

$$t + 7 - 7 = 2 - 7$$

Do the **opposite** of **+ 7**. **Subtract 7** from **both** sides.

$$t = -5$$

Check that the solution works: $-5 + 7 = 2$ ✓

 ISBN: 9780170447492

Solve the following, showing all the steps in the working. Then check your answers.

1 $a + 4 = 10$

_____ = _____

a = _____

Check: 6 + 4 = 10 ✓

2 $b - 7 = 12$

_____ = _____

b = _____

Check: _____ – 7 = 12 ☐

3 $c - 6 = 20$

_____ = _____

c = _____

Check: _____ – 6 = 20 ☐

4 $d + 9 = 13$

_____ = _____

d = _____

Check: _____ + 9 = 13 ☐

5 $e - 11 = 22$

_____ = _____

e = _____

Check: _____ – 11 = 22 ☐

6 $f - 5 = 0$

_____ = _____

f = _____

Check: _____ – 5 = 0 ☐

7 $g + 15 = 18$

____

____

Check: _____ + 15 = 18 ☐

8 $h + 6 = 2$

____

____

Check: _____ + 6 = 2 ☐

9 $i + 12 = 0$

____

____

Check: _____ + 12 = 0 ☐

10 $j - 1 = -9$

____

____

Check: _____ – 1 = –9 ☐

A trick:
Sometimes the **variable** is on the **right**-hand side. Example: $5 = y + 3$.
Because both sides are equal to each other, you can **flip** them around:

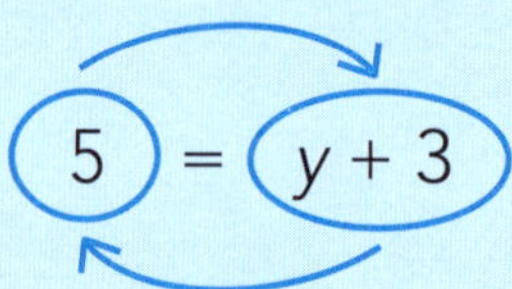

so $y + 3 = 5$

Check the remaining answers in your head.

11 $9 = v - 5$

________ = ________

12 $5 = s + 1$

________ = ________

13 $11 = p - 3$

14 $-7 = t - 6$

15 $-20 = u + 15$

16 $-13 = w - 2$

17 $10 = -5 + a$

18 $-12 = 7 + b$

 ISBN: 9780170447492

Another trick:
Sometimes the **variable** has a **negative sign**. Example: $9 - p = 13$.

$$9 - p = 13$$
$$9 - 9 - p = 13 - 9$$
$$-p = 4$$
$$-p \times -1 = 4 \times -1$$
$$p = -4$$

Remember: this – sign belongs to the p, not the 9.

We need to get rid of the + 9 from the left side.

Do the **opposite** of **+ 9**. **Subtract 9** from **both** sides.

Trick: **Multiply both sides** by **–1**.

Check that the solution works: $9 - (-4) = 13$ ✓

19 $12 - z = 10$

20 $9 - q = 12$

21 $r - 18 = 0$

22 $24 - k = 14$

23 $15 - n = -1$

24 $20 = 36 - m$

25 $50 = -7 - d$

26 $-8 = -12 - g$

27 $-19 = 4 - y$

28 $-5 - w = 13$

ISBN: 9780170447492

Find the errors

Some of the following equations are solved correctly and some aren't. If the equation is solved correctly, put a tick in the ✓/✗ column. If not, put a cross in the ✓/✗ column, highlight the mistake, and write the correct answer.

		✓/✗	Correct solution
1	$p+7=2$ $p+7+7=2+7$ $p=9$		
2	$h-8=2$ $h-8+8=2+8$ $h=10$		
3	$z-9=-4$ $z-9+9=-4$ $z=-4$		
4	$w+13=-6$ $w+13-13=-6-13$ $w=19$		
5	$8-v=3$ $8-v-8=3-8$ $-v=-5$ $v=5$		
6	$19=-12-w$ $19+12=-w$ $31=-w$ $w=-31$		

 ISBN: 9780170447492

Multiplying and dividing

Examples:

1 $\frac{d}{4} = 5$

We need to get rid of the ÷ 4 from the left side.

$\frac{d}{4} \times \frac{4}{1} = 5 \times 4$

Do the **opposite** of ÷ 4. **Multiply both** sides by 4 (or $\frac{4}{1}$ if you are dealing with fractions).

$d = 20$

Check that the solution works: $\frac{20}{4} = 5$ ✓

2 $5f = 20$

Remember, $5f$ means $5 \times f$. We need to get rid of the x 5 from the left side.

$\frac{5f}{5} = \frac{20}{5}$

Do the **opposite** of x 5. **Divide both** sides by 5.

$f = 4$

Check that the solution works: $5 \times 4 = 20$ ✓

Solve the following, showing all the steps in the working.

1 $\frac{a}{2} = 7$

______ = ______

$a =$ ______

Check: $\frac{\_\_\_}{2} = 7$ ☐

2 $3 \times b = 18$

______ = ______

$b =$ ______

Check: $3 \times$ ______ $= 18$ ☐

3 $8c = 24$

______ = ______

$c =$ ______

Check: $8 \times$ ______ $= 24$ ☐

4 $\frac{d}{5} = 20$

______ = ______

$d =$ ______

Check: $\frac{\_\_\_}{5} = 20$ ☐

ISBN: 9780170447492

5 $7e = 42$

_______ = _______

$e =$ _______

Check: $7 \times$ _____ $= 42$ ☐

6 $\frac{f}{9} = 3$

_______ = _______

$f =$ _______

Check: $\frac{\_\_\_\_}{9} = 3$ ☐

7 $\frac{g}{6} = -2$

_______ = _______

$g =$ _______

Check: $\frac{\_\_\_\_}{6} = -2$ ☐

8 $4h = 32$

_______ = _______

$h =$ _______

Check: $4 \times$ _____ $= 32$ 

9 $5i = -35$

____

____

Check: $5 \times$ _____ $= -35$ ☐

10 $j \div 4 = 25$

____

____

Check: _____ $\div 4 = 25$ 

11 $3k = 90$

____

____

Check: $3 \times$ _____ $= 90$ ☐

12 $15m = -45$

____

____

Check: $15 \times$ _____ $= -45$ ☐

13 $\frac{n}{10} = -8$

____

____

Check: $\frac{\_\_\_\_}{10} = -8$ ☐

14 $p \div 11 = -5$

____

____

Check: _____ $\div 11 = -5$ ☐

 ISBN: 9780170447492

The tricks again:

- If the **variable** is on the **right**-hand side, **flip** the sides around.
- If the variable is **negative**, multiply **both sides by –1**.

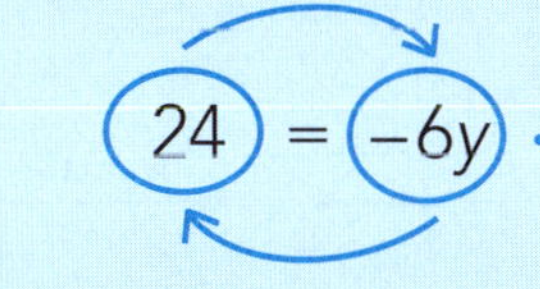

Flip the sides around.

so $-6y = 24$

$$\frac{-6y}{6} = \frac{24}{6}$$

$$-1 \times -y = 4 \times -1$$

Multiply both sides by –1.

$$y = -4$$

Check that the solution works: $24 = -6 \times -4$ ✓

Check the remaining answers in your head.

15 $30 = \frac{q}{4}$

16 $-10 = 5r$

17 $\frac{-s}{4} = 6$

18 $-8 = \frac{-t}{2}$

19 $-4 = u \div -9$

20 $-7 = w \div 2$

ISBN: 9780170447492

Mixing it up

1 $a - 9 = 17$

2 $\frac{b}{4} = 8$

3 $50 = 5c$

4 $\frac{-d}{10} = 20$

5 $48 = e + 6$

6 $-7 = f \div 7$

7 $-100 = 40 + g$

8 $h \div 9 = -1$

9 $\frac{-i}{2} = 6$

10 $-6j = 480$

 ISBN: 9780170447492

Challenge 3

Do the working needed to complete the cross-number in your exercise book.

	1	2		3		
4						5
6			7		8	
		9				
10					11	12
		13		14		
	15			16		

Across		Down	
1	$x + 3 = 24$	**2**	$10 = x - 7$
3	$2x = 62$	**3**	$\frac{x}{3} = 13$
6	$7 = \frac{x}{6}$	**4**	$x \div 8 = 8$
8	$42 = -9 + x$	**5**	$9 = x \div 9$
9	$1200 = 12x$	**7**	$202 = x + 101$
10	$29 = x + 4$	**10**	$\frac{-x}{6} = -4$
11	$3 = \frac{x}{25}$	**12**	$x - 19 = 32$
15	$39 = x + 10$	**13**	$-7 = x \div -7$
16	$4 = \frac{x}{15}$	**14**	$-32 = -2x$

ISBN: 9780170447492

Forming then solving equations

- You need to be able to translate expressions written using words into mathematical expressions.
- On page 10 you learned some of the symbols that can represent words.
- All of the following terms can be translated to an 'equals' sign.

'equals'	=
'is'	
'to get'	
'makes'	
'comes to'	
'totals'	
'add up to'	

Write an equation for each of the following, and then solve it to find the mystery number. Use the variable *n* to represent the number.

1 Multiply a number by three to get eighteen.

$3n = 18$

$\frac{3n}{} = \frac{18}{}$

$n =$

2 Divide a number by two to get twenty.

3 A number plus ten makes seventeen.

4 Five less than a number comes to nine.

 ISBN: 9780170447492

5 A number shared equally between two is twelve.

6 A number multiplied by six is twelve.

7 Double a number makes sixteen.

8 A number divided by three is twelve.

9 Three less than a number comes to nine.

10 A four added to a number totals ten.

11 Three, four and a number add up to nine.

12 Half a number is five.

13 Five less than a number is eight.

14 Three times a number is fifteen.

ISBN: 9780170447492

Understanding instructions in algebra

How do I recognise when to ...?	Example	What do I do?	What should the answer look like?
Simplify	Adding/ Subtracting $a + b + a + 5$ Contains a mixture of like and unlike terms.	Combine like terms. $a + b + a + 5$ $= 2a + b + 5$	An expression containing no like terms. e.g. $2a + b + 5$
	Multiplying $3b \times 2b$ The same variable occurs in more than one place.	Multiply the coefficients and multiply the variables. $3b \times 2b = 6b^2$	An expression in which each variable occurs no more than once. e.g. $6b^2$
	Dividing $\frac{4b}{24}$ The numerator and denominator have a common factor (4).	Divide the numerator and denominator by the common factor. $\frac{4b}{24} = \frac{b}{6}$	
Evaluate (substitute)	$x + 3$ when $x = 7$ You are told the value of a variable.	Substitute the value for the variable. $x + 3 = 7 + 3$ $= 10$	A constant. e.g. 10
Solve	$5 +$ © $= 9$ When you have an unknown symbol or letter.	Find the value of a symbol or letter. $5 +$ © $= 9$ © $= 4$	Variable = constant. © $= 4$

 ISBN: 9780170447492

Write the most appropriate instruction (**Simplify**, **Evaluate** or **Solve**) for each question. Then follow your chosen instruction in order to answer the question.

	Question	Instruction	Answer
1	$10 - a = 3$		
2	$p + t + 2p$		
3	$8b \times 2b$		
4	$\frac{12y}{4}$		
5	$3x + 6 - x$		
6	$4x + 2$ when $x = 3$		
7	$6d = -12$		
8	$\frac{10v^2}{v}$		
9	$3h^2$ if $h = 2$		
10	$\frac{g}{9} = -3$		

ISBN: 9780170447492

Patterns

- Patterns can be seen all around us, often in art and cultural decorations.

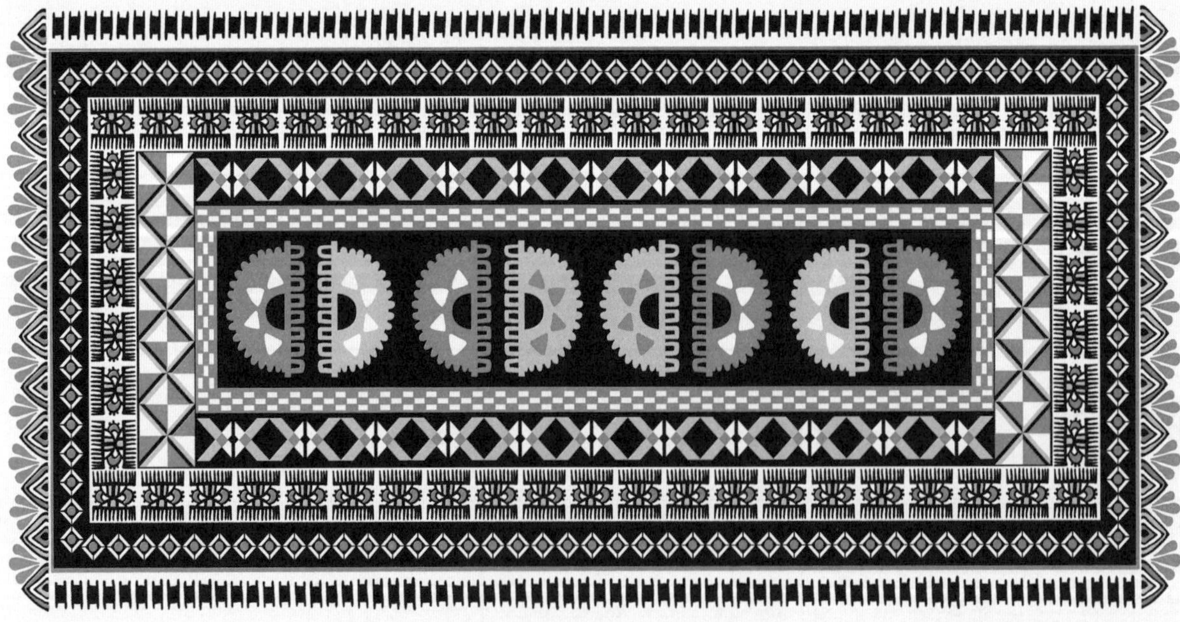

- When investigating patterns, it is easiest to use objects such as popsicle sticks to represent straight lines, buttons to represent dots, etc.

ISBN: 9780170447492

Continuing patterns

- You need to work out how patterns change so you can draw more shapes.

Draw the next shape for each of these patterns.

1

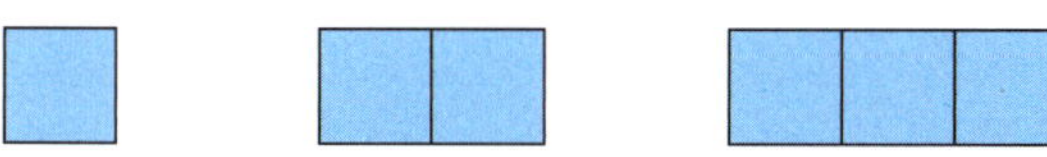

2

3

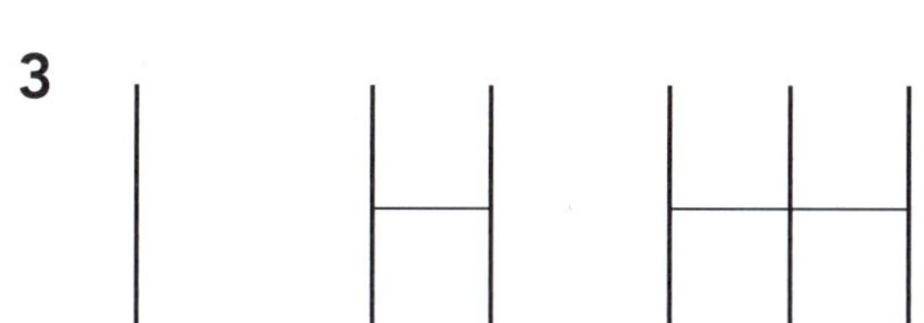

4

5

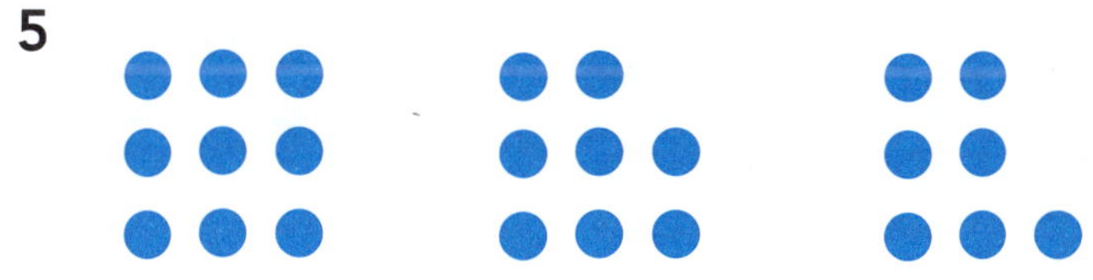

6

7

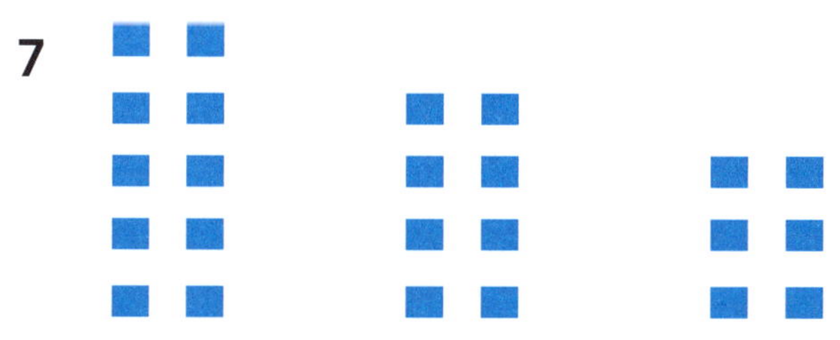

ISBN: 9780170447492

From pictures to numbers

Write down the number of objects that are in each of these shapes.

1 Number of stars

2 ____ 4 ____ ____ ____ ____

2 Number of dots

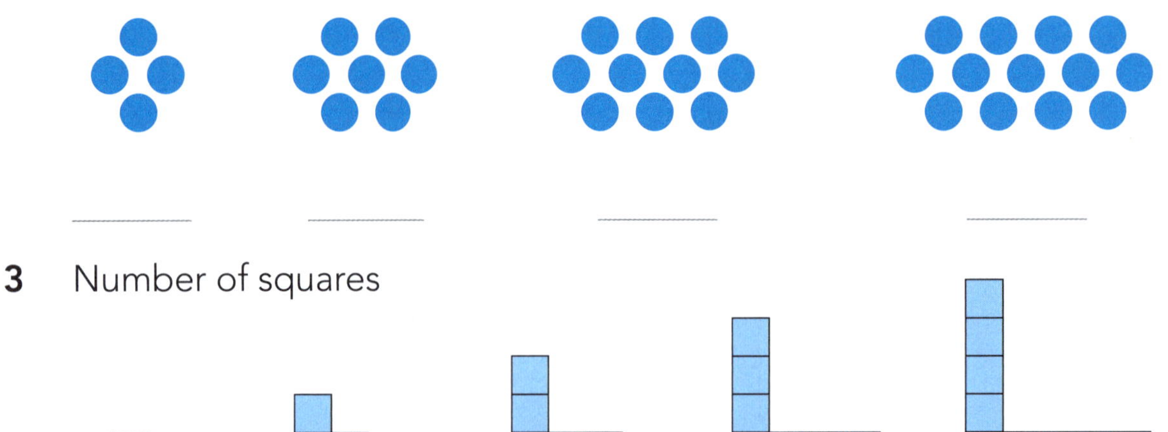

____ ____ ____ ____

3 Number of squares

____ ____ ____ ____ ____

4 Number of squares

____ ____ ____ ____

5 Number of dots

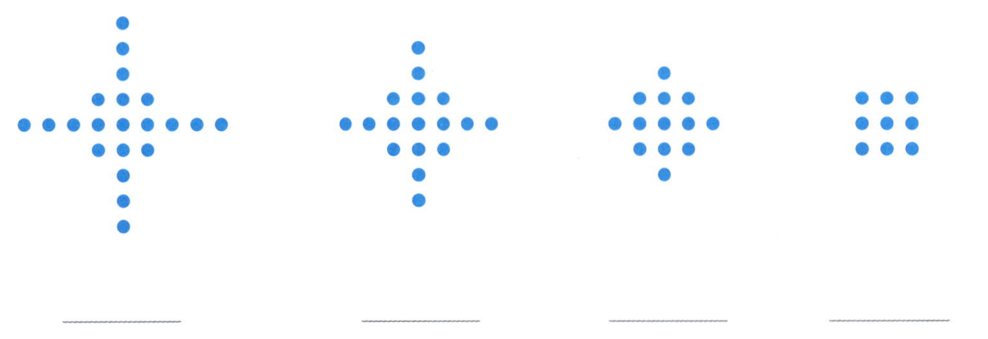

____ ____ ____ ____

 ISBN: 9780170447492

Describing patterns

Fill in the gaps to complete the descriptions of these patterns.

1

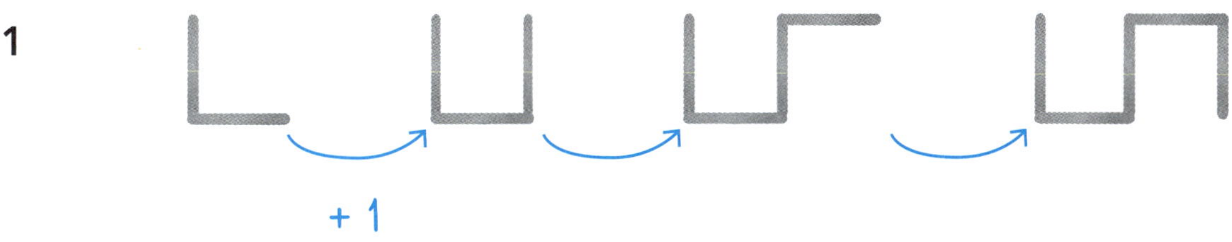

I started with ______ **popsicle sticks** and then I **added 1** each time.

2

I started with ______ **dots** and then I **added** ______ each time.

3

I started with ______ **crosses** and then I **added** ______ each time.

4

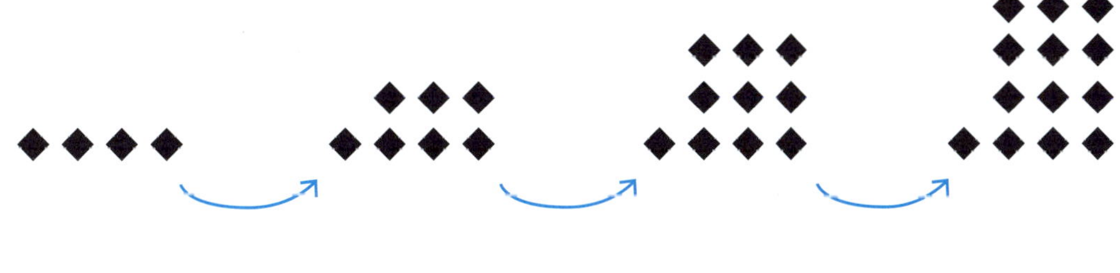

I started with ______ **diamonds** and then I **added** ______ each time.

5 

– 2 _____ _____

I started with _____ **popsicle sticks** ____________________

____.

6 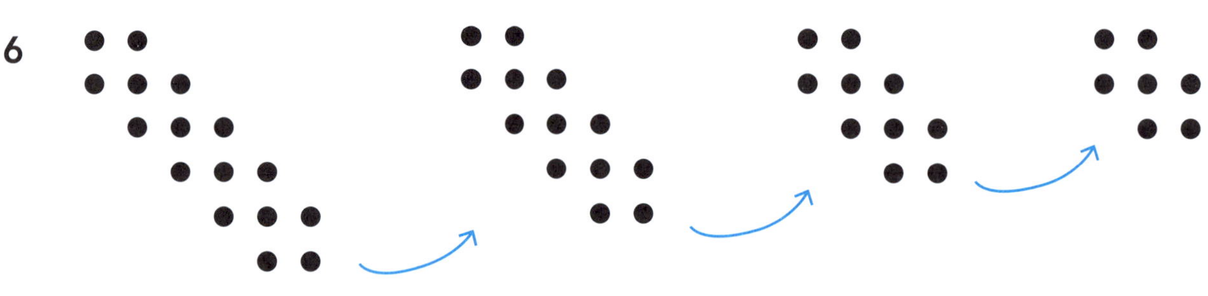

_____ _____ _____

I started with _____ **dots** ____________________

____.

7 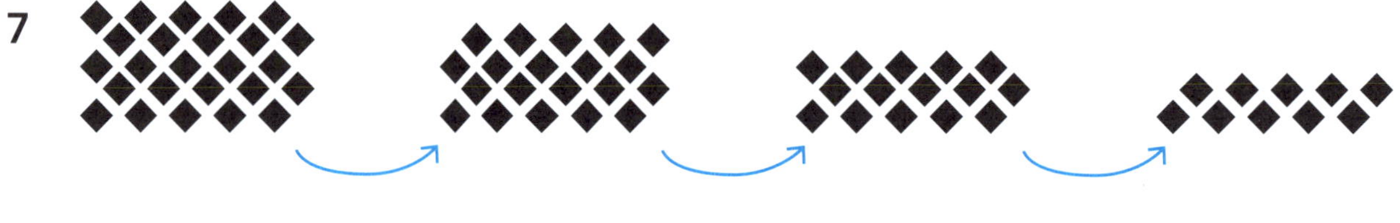

_____ _____ _____

____

____.

8 × × × × ×   × × × × ×   × × × × ×   × × × × ×
× × × × ×   × × × ×   × × ×   × ×

_____ _____ _____

____

____.

ISBN: 9780170447492

Patterns into tables

- Tables are a very useful way of showing patterns.
- We can use tables:
  - — to show us the pattern, and
  - — to predict, for instance, the number of popsicle sticks needed for bigger shapes **without having to draw them**.

Example:

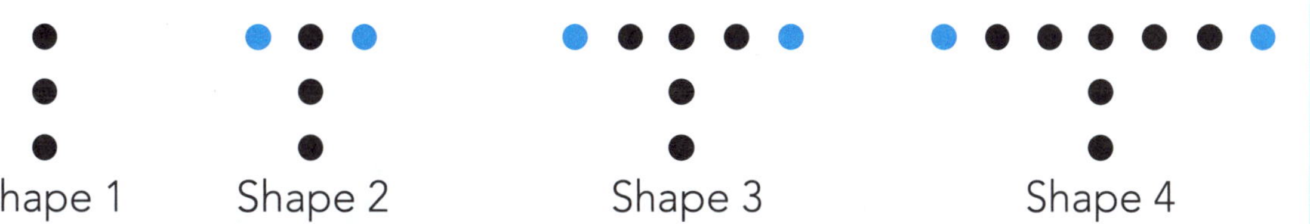

Shape number	Number of dots
1	3
2	5
3	7
4	9
5	**11**
6	**13**

+ 2 + 2 + 2 + 2 + 2

To find the number in the next term, we need to **add 2**. You can see this in the shapes: **2 more** dots were added each time.

Because we added 2 for the first row, we **keep adding 2** to complete the table — **without** having to draw the pictures.

Draw the arrows and complete the tables for the shapes that have been drawn (the white boxes). Then, without drawing the next shapes, fill in the grey boxes.

1

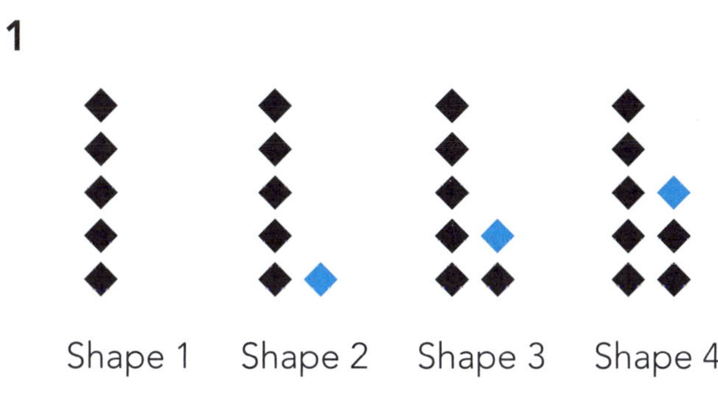

Shape number	Number of diamonds
1	5
2	
3	
4	
5	
6	

2

Shape 1 Shape 2 Shape 3 Shape 4

Shape number	1	2	3	4	5	6
Number of crosses	1	4				

3

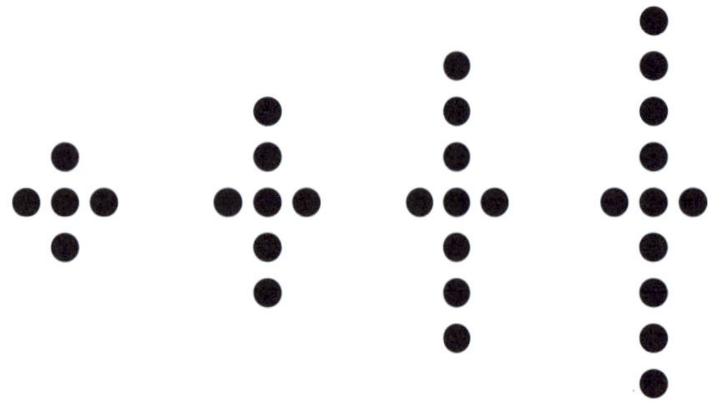

Shape 1 Shape 2 Shape 3 Shape 4

Shape number	Number of dots
1	5
2	
3	
4	
5	
6	

4

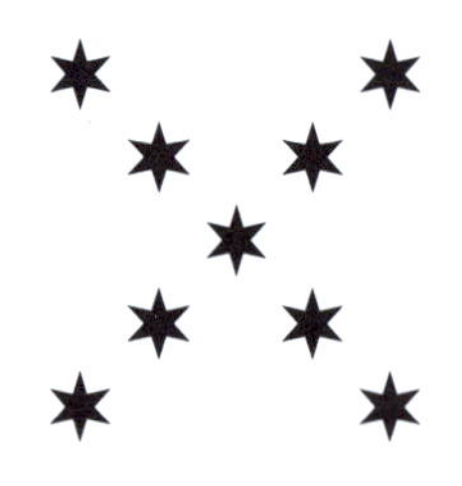

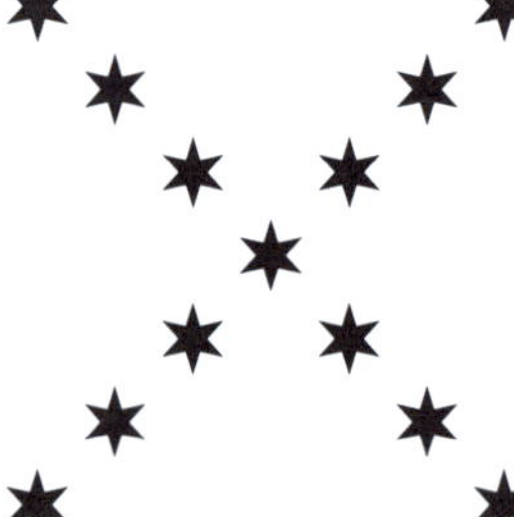

Shape 1 Shape 2 Shape 3 Shape 4

Shape number	1	2	3	4	5	6
Number of stars	1					

 ISBN: 9780170447492

5

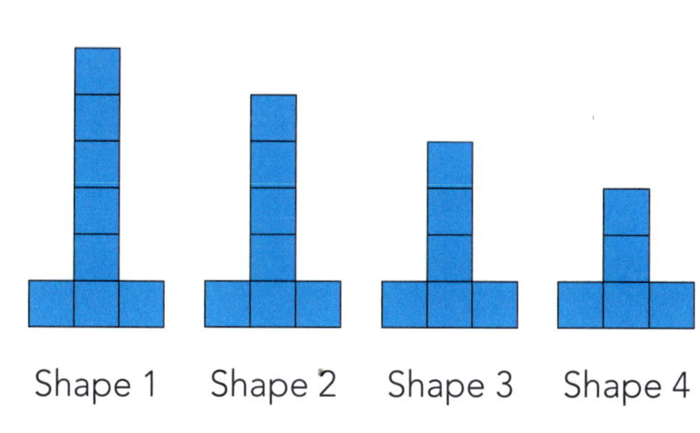

Shape number	Number of squares
1	8
2	
3	
4	
5	
6	

6

Shape 1 Shape 2 Shape 3

Shape number	1	2	3	4	5	6
Number of crosses		14				

7

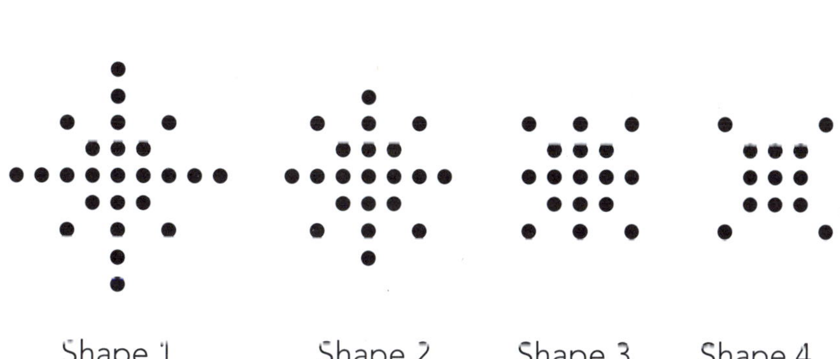

Shape number	Number of dots
1	
2	
3	
4	
5	

ISBN: 9780170447492

Finding term 'zero'

- Not all patterns involve **shapes**, e.g. the odd numbers between 10 and 20 form a pattern: 11, 13, 15, 17, 19.
- So from now on we will use the word '**term**' instead of 'shape'.
- It will also be very useful to find the **value of term 0**.

Example:

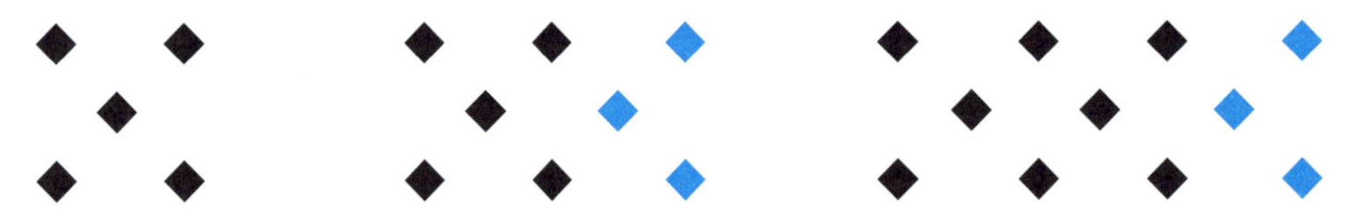

Term number	Number of diamonds
0	**2**
1	5
2	8
3	11
4	14

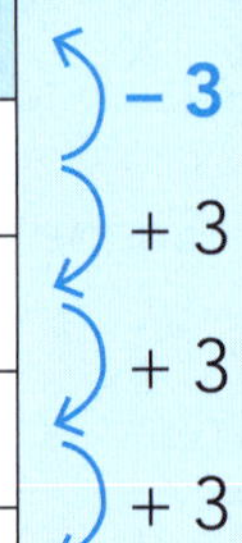

To find the bigger terms we **add three**. So to find term zero we need to **subtract three** from the first term.

5 **– 3** = 2

Complete the tables, including the value for term zero.

1

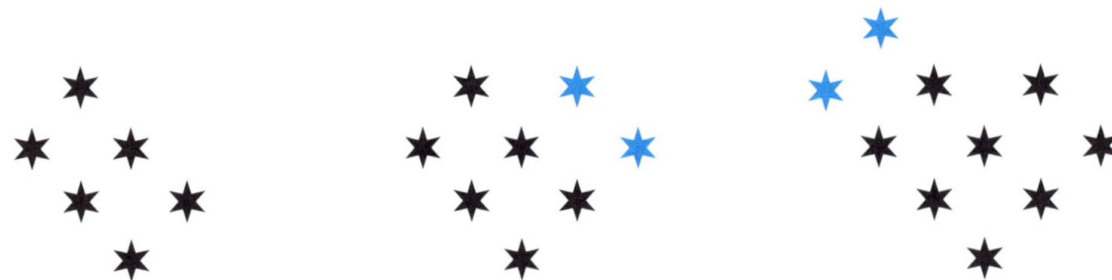

Term number	0	1	2	3	4	5	6
Number of stars		6					

ISBN: 9780170447492

2

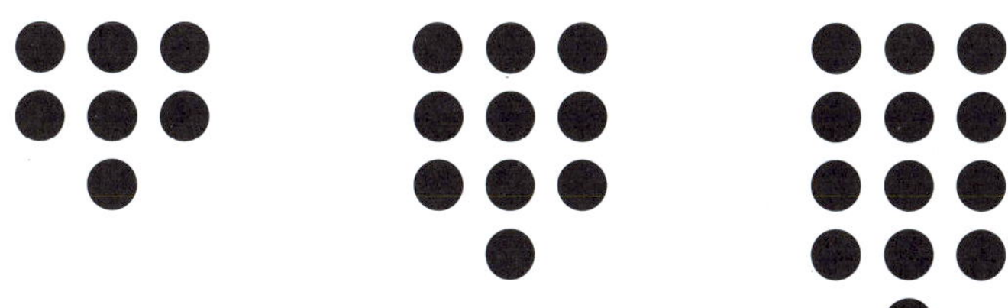

Term number	Number of dots
0	
1	
2	10
3	
4	
5	

3

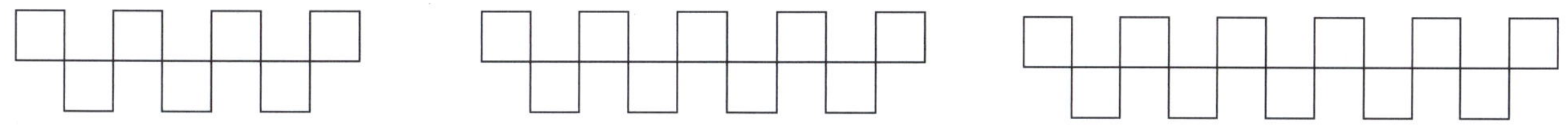

Term number	0	1	2	3	4	5	6
Number of squares							

4

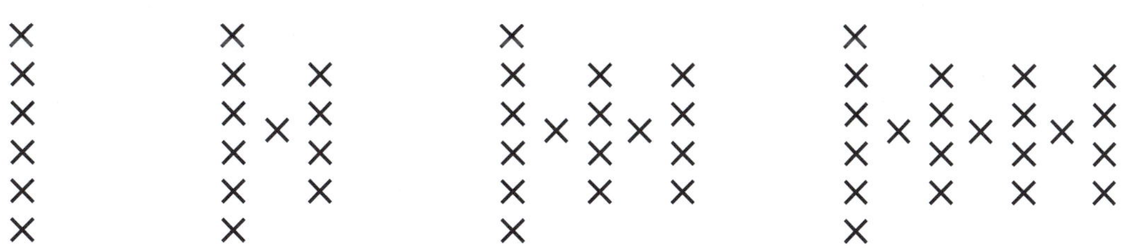

Term number	0	1	2	3	4	5	6
Number of crosses							

ISBN: 9780170447492

5

Term number	Number of diamonds
0	
1	
2	
3	
4	
5	

6

Term number	0	1	2	3	4	5	6
Number of small triangles							

7

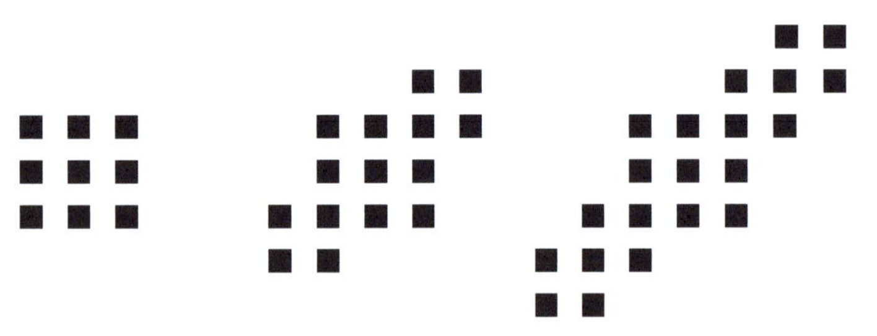

Term number	Number of squares
0	
1	
2	
3	
4	
5	

 ISBN: 9780170447492

Finding the rule from shapes and a table

- It is useful to have a **mathematical rule** for patterns so we can work out, for instance, the value of the 100th term **without** having to draw pictures or create a large table.
- Mathematical rules are easiest if they are written using **letters** (which we call **variables**), rather than words.

Examples:

1

Term number (n)	Number of diamonds (D)
0	1
1	5
2	9
3	13
4	17
5	21

−4, +4, +4, +4, +4

We could draw shape number 0: it would be just 1 diamond. ◆

Remember, do the **opposite** (−4) to find term 0.

In words: The first term has ___five___ diamonds and then I added ___four___ each time.

Find the rule: Number of **D**iamonds = ___4___ x term **n**umber ___+ 1___

This is the number of diamonds that you need for **term number 0**.

Tidy it up: $D = 4n + 1$

Use **D** to represent the number of **D**iamonds.

Use **n** to represent the term **n**umber.

Word rule: The number of **D**iamonds is calculated by multiplying the term **n**umber by **four** and then **adding one**.

ISBN: 9780170447492

Use the rule:

2 To find the number of diamonds needed for the **10th** shape:

$n = 10$, so $\quad D = 4n + 1$

$= 4 \times 10 + 1$

$= 41$

We have found the number of diamonds needed for the 10th shape **without** having to draw all the shapes or create a bigger table.

This is what it would look like:

It is much quicker to calculate the number of diamonds needed for big shapes, than to draw them.

Another way of finding term 0.

Term number (n)	Number of diamonds (D)		4 times table
0	1	← + 1	0
1	5		4
2	9	+ 4	8
3	13	+ 4	12
4	17	+ 4	16
5	21	+ 4	20

1 We **added 4** each time, so write the **4 times table.**

+ 1

2 To get the 4 times table to the number of diamonds (D), we have to **add 1** each time.

So, $D = 4n + 1$

 ISBN: 9780170447492

Complete the tables and fill in the gaps.

1

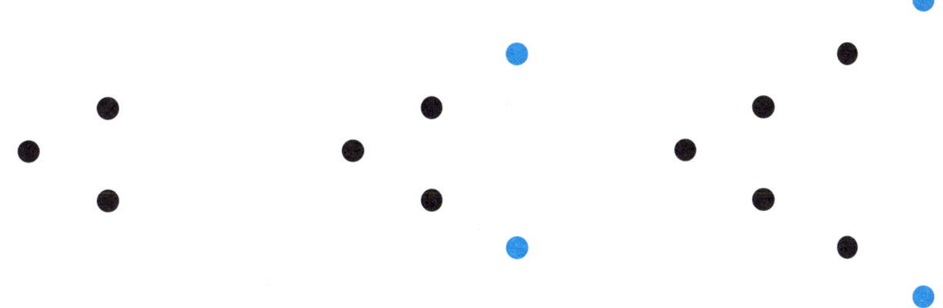

Complete the table:

Term number (n)	Number of dots (D)
0	
1	3
2	
3	
4	
5	

In words:
The first term has ________ dots and then I added ________ each time.

Find the mathematical rule:

Number of dots = ________ x term number + ________

Tidy it up: $D =$ ________ $n +$ ________

Word rule:
The number of dots is calculated by multiplying the term number by ________ and then adding ________.

Use the rule:
How many dots would be needed for the 20th shape?

$D =$ ________ x 20 ________

= ________________

= ________

ISBN: 9780170447492

2

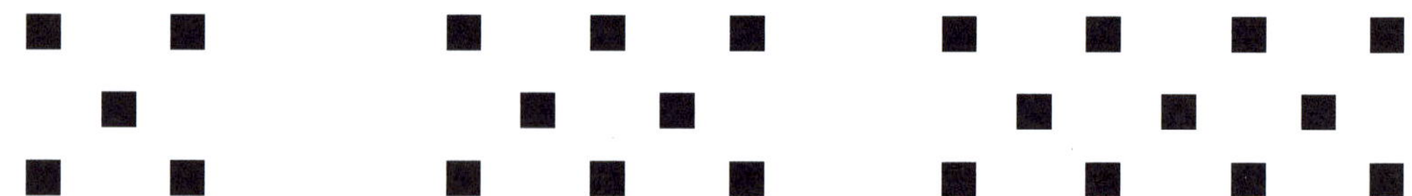

Complete the table:

Term number (n)	Number of squares (S)
0	
1	5
2	
3	
4	
5	

______

In words:
The first term has ________ squares and then I added ________ each time.

Find the mathematical rule:

Number of squares = ________ x term number + ________

Tidy it up: S = ________ n + ________

Word rule:
The number of squares is calculated by multiplying the term number by ________ and then adding ________.

Use the rule:
How many squares would be needed for the 30th shape?

S = ________________

= ________________

= ________

 ISBN: 9780170447492

3

  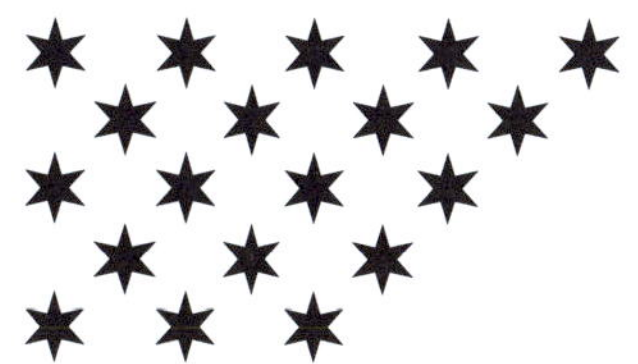

Complete the table:

Term number (n)	Number of stars (S)
0	
1	9
2	
3	
4	
5	

In words:
The first term has ________ stars and then I added ________ each time.

Find the mathematical rule:

Number of stars = ________ x term number + ________

Tidy it up: S = ________n + ________

Word rule:
The number of stars is calculated by multiplying the term number by ________ and then adding ________.

Use the rule:
How many stars would be needed for the 25th shape?

S = ____________________

= ____________________

= ____________

ISBN: 9780170447492

4

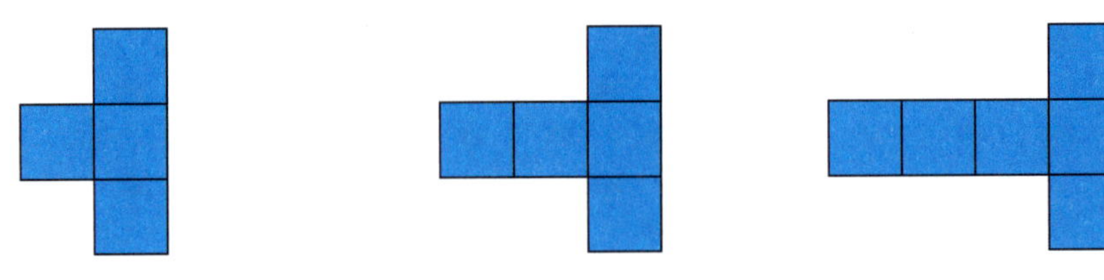

Complete the table:

Term number (n)	Number of squares (S)
0	
1	4
2	
3	
4	
5	

In words:
The first term has ________ squares and then I added ________ each time.

Find the mathematical rule:

Number of squares = ________ x term number + ________

Tidy it up: $S =$ ________ $n +$ ________

Word rule:
The number of squares is calculated by multiplying the term number by ________ and then adding ________.

Use the rule:
How many squares would be needed for the 35th shape?

$S =$ ____________________

$=$ ____________________

$=$ ____________

 ISBN: 9780170447492

5

```
×   ×        ×   ×   ×          ×   ×   ×   ×
× × ×        × × × × ×          × × × × × × ×
×   ×        ×   ×   ×          ×   ×   ×   ×
```

Complete the table:

Term number (n)	Number of crosses (C)
0	
1	7
2	
3	
4	
5	

In words:
The first term has ________ crosses and then I added ________ each time.

Find the mathematical rule:

Number of crosses = ________ x term number + ________

Tidy it up: C = ________ n + ________

Word rule:
The number of crosses is calculated by multiplying the term number by ________ and then adding ________.

Use the rule:
How many crosses would be needed for the 50th shape?

C – ____________________

= ____________________

= ________

ISBN: 9780170447492

Finding the rule from a description

- As we said earlier, not all patterns involve shapes: patterns are sometimes described.
- In these cases we need to use the description to draw a table.

Examples:

1 Odd numbers that are bigger than four.

Draw a table:

Term number (n)	Value of term (T)
0	3
1	5
2	7
3	9
4	11

– 2, + 2, + 2, + 2

Find the rule:

The pattern **increases** by **two** each time.

$T = 2 \times n + 3$

This is the value of term zero.

Tidy it up:

$T = 2n + 3$

Use the rule:

Find the 50th odd number that is bigger than four.

$T = 2n + 3$
$= 2 \times 50 + 3$
$= 103$

2 Multiples of four that are greater than ten.

Draw a table:

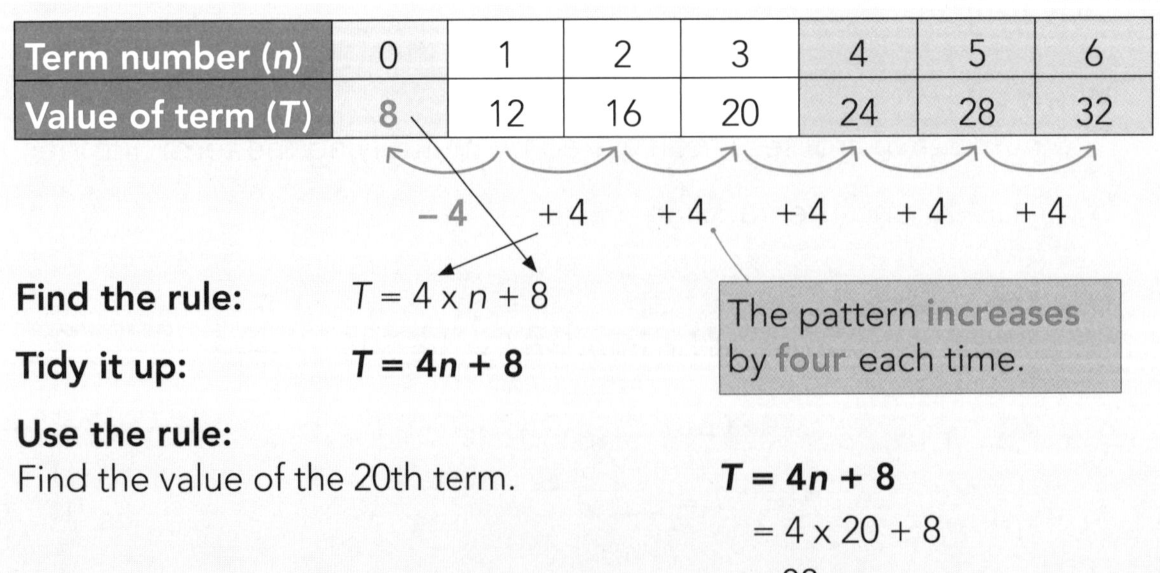

Term number (n)	0	1	2	3	4	5	6
Value of term (T)	8	12	16	20	24	28	32

– 4, + 4, + 4, + 4, + 4, + 4

Find the rule: $T = 4 \times n + 8$

Tidy it up: $T = 4n + 8$

The pattern **increases** by **four** each time.

Use the rule:

Find the value of the 20th term.

$T = 4n + 8$
$= 4 \times 20 + 8$
$= 88$

ISBN: 9780170447492

Complete the tables and find the rules for the following.

1 Start at five and go up in threes.

Term number (n)	Value of term (T)
0	
1	5
2	8
3	
4	
5	

Rule: T = ______ n + ______

2 Even numbers bigger than seven.

Term number (n)	0	1	2	3	4	5
Value of term (T)		8				

Rule: T = ______ n + ______

3 Multiples of five that are bigger than nine.

Term number (n)	Value of term (T)
0	
1	
2	
3	
4	
5	

Rule: T = ______ n + ______

4 Start at thirteen and go up in fours.

Term number (n)	0	1	2	3	4	5
Value of term (T)						

Rule: T = ______ n + ______

5 Multiples of three that are bigger than ten.

Term number (n)	Value of term (T)
0	
1	
2	
3	
4	
5	

Rule:

$T =$ ______ $n +$ ______

6 Even numbers that are bigger than fifteen.

Term number (n)	0	1	2	3	4	5
Value of term (T)						

Rule: $T =$ ______ $n +$ ______

7 Multiples of three that are bigger than two.

Term number (n)	Value of term (T)

Rule:

$T =$ ______ $n +$ ______

8 Odd numbers that are bigger than two.

Term number (n)						
Value of term (T)						

Rule: $T =$ ______ $n +$ ______

 ISBN: 9780170447492

Notice that there is no column or row for term 0 in these examples. You will still need to work out its value.

9 Even numbers that are bigger than fifteen.

Rule:

Term number (n)	1	2	3	4
Value of term (T)				

$T =$ ______

10 Answers to the nine times table, starting from nine.

Rule:

Term number (n)	Value of term (T)
1	
2	
3	
4	
5	

$T =$ ______

11 Multiples of ten that are bigger than ninety-nine.

Rule:

Term number (n)	1	2	3	4	5
Value of term (T)					

$T =$ ______

12 Whole numbers of dozens.

Rule:

Term number (n)	Value of term (T)
1	
2	
3	
4	
5	

$T =$ ______

ISBN: 9780170447492

Finding the rule from a list

- You can find a rule from a table, but finding a rule from just a list saves space and time.

Example:

Term number (n)	0	1	2	3	4	5
Value of term (T)	**5**	7	9	11	13	15

Notice you are not given **term 0**.

Instead of the table, you would be given: 7, 9, 11, 13, 15, ...

This means that the pattern goes on for ever.

Pattern:

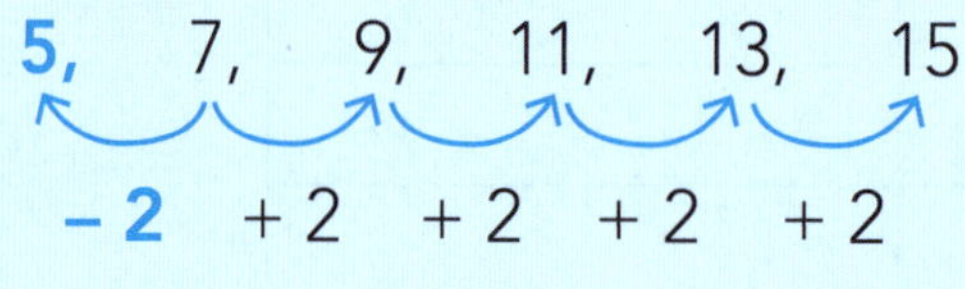

As usual, find the pattern (+ 2), and do the **opposite** **(– 2)** to find **term 0**.

Find the rule: $T = 2n + 5$

Remember, this is the value of **term zero**.

Words: Any value in the pattern can be calculated by multiplying the term number by **two** and then adding **five**.

Complete the statements and find the rule for each of these.

1 ____, 5, 6, 7, 8, ...

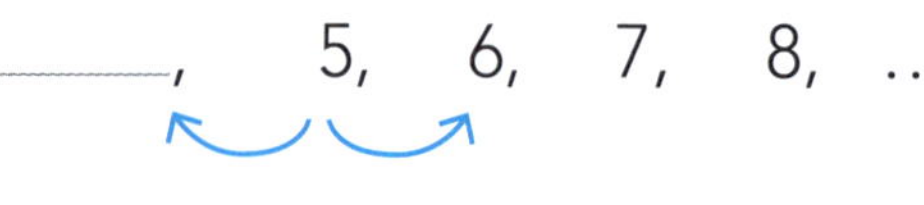

____ ____

Rule:

$T =$ ____ $n +$ ____

The first term has 5 and then I added ____ each time.

Term zero will be ____.

2 ____, 6, 9, 12, 15, ...

____ ____

Rule:

$T =$ ____ $n +$ ____

The first term has ____ and then I added ____ each time.

Term zero will be ____.

 ISBN: 9780170447492

3 ______, 9, 13, 17, 21, 25, … Rule:

______ ______ $T =$ ______$n +$ ______

The first term has ____ and then I added ____ each time.

Term zero will be ______.

4 ______, 11, 13, 15, 17, … Rule:

______ ______ $T =$ ______$n +$ ______

The first term has ____ and then I added ____ each time.

Term zero will be ______.

5 ______, 7, 12, 17, 22, 27, … Rule:

The first term has ____ and then I added ____ each time. $T =$ ______$n +$ ______

Term zero will be ______.

6 ______, 11, 15, 19, 23, 27, … Rule:

The first term has ____ and then I added ____ each time. $T =$ ____________

Term zero will be ______.

7 ______, 15, 18, 21, 24, 27, … Rule:

The first term has ____ and then I added ____ each time. $T =$ ____________

Term zero will be ______.

8 6, 10, 14, 18, 22, … Rule:

$T =$ ____________

9 14, 16, 18, 20, 22, … Rule:

$T =$ ____________

10 5, 8, 11, 14, 17, … Rule:

$T =$ ____________

ISBN: 9780170447492

Applications

- There are many practical situations where it's useful to find the rule.
- From now on, we will use the term **sequence**, rather than pattern.
- A sequence is a list of numbers or objects **in a particular order**.
- Sometime sequences occur in everyday situations.

Example: Gloria has \$9 in her bank account and saves \$5 each week. Find the rule for calculating the total in her account after n weeks.

Write a list for the sequence: \$9, \$14, \$19, \$24, \$29, …

To find the rule you would need to work out the zero term:

\$4, \$9, \$14, \$19, \$24, \$29, …

– 5

Rule: $T = 5n + 4$

Create a list and then find the rule for each of these descriptions.

1 Henare has \$24 in his bank account, and he saves \$10 each week. Find the rule for calculating the total in his account after n weeks.

$T =$ ____ $n +$ ____

\$24, ____, ____, ____, ____,

2 Charlie runs 2 km in his first week of training. He increases this by 1 km each week. Find the rule for calculating the distance he runs during his nth week of training.

$T =$ ____ $n +$ ____

____, ____, ____, ____, ____,

3 When Annie babysits, she is paid \$10, plus \$12 for each hour. Find the rule for calculating her total pay for babysitting for n hours.

$T =$ ____ $n +$ ____

____, ____, ____, ____, ____,

ISBN: 9780170447492

4 **a** Marama wants to hire a dinghy and go for a row. Dodgy Dinghies charges \$10 plus \$5 for each hour. Find the rule for calculating the total cost of hiring the dinghy for n hours.

$T =$ ________

____, ____, ____, ____, ____,

b Dicey Dinghies charges \$5 plus \$7 for each hour. Find the rule for calculating the total cost of hiring the dinghy for n hours.

$T =$ ________

____, ____, ____, ____, ____,

c Which hire company should she choose if she wants to hire a dinghy for three hours? Explain your answer.

____

____

5 Tatty Taxis charges \$15 plus \$3 for each kilometre. Find the rule for calculating the total fare for a journey of n kilometres.

$T =$ ____ $n +$ ____

____, ____, ____, ____, ____,

6 Grandma is collecting the stickers offered by her local supermarket. When she pays for her groceries she gets four stickers each week. Find the rule for calculating the total number of stickers after n weeks.

$T =$ ________

____, ____, ____, ____, ____,

7 An electrician charges \$30 for her travel time, plus \$65 for each hour of work. Find the rule for calculating the total cost for her services for n hours of work.

$T =$ ________

____, ____, ____, ____, ____,

8 Elijah wants to buy an outdoor dining table and some chairs. The table costs \$599, and each chair is \$159. Find the rule for calculating the total cost for a table and n chairs.

$T =$ ________

ISBN: 9780170447492

Finding a term from a rule

- We can use the rule to find the value of any term in the sequence.
- This is much faster than writing a list.

Examples:

1 Find the 20th term for the sequence that has the rule $T = 2n + 3$.

$$T = 2n + 3$$
$$= 2 \times \mathbf{20} + 3$$
$$= 43$$

Substitute **20** for ***n***.

2 Find the 15th term for the sequence that has the rule $T = 3n + 5$.

$$T = 3n + 5$$
$$= 3 \times \mathbf{15} + 5$$
$$= 50$$

Use the rules to calculate the terms.

1 30th term $T = 4n + 1$

= ____________________

= ____________

2 20th term $T = 2n + 5$

= ____________________

= ____________

3 40th term $T = 3n + 4$

= ____________________

= ____________

4 20th term $T = n + 10$

= ____________________

= ____________

5 15th term $T = 6n + 2$

= ____________________

= ____________

6 10th term $T = 3n + 4$

= ____________________

= ____________

ISBN: 9780170447492

7 10th term $T = 4n + 8$

$= $ ______

$= $ ______

8 9th term $T = 7n + 4$

$= $ ______

$= $ ______

9 14th term $T = 3n + 1$

$= $ ______

$= $ ______

10 18th term $T = 10n + 2$

$= $ ______

$= $ ______

11 **a** Manaia works out that the equation for the total cost (\$) (T) of hiring a canoe for n hours from Crafty Canoes is: $T = 10n + 5$

How much is the hourly cost for hiring a canoe?

______

b Use the equation to calculate the cost of hiring a canoe for seven hours.

______

12 **a** Toby is preparing folders of information for members of his club. The equation for calculating the total cost (\$) (T) of a folder containing n pages is: $T = 0.02n + 1.99$

How much does an empty folder cost?

______

b Use the equation to calculate the total cost of printing a folder containing forty pages.

______

13 **a** Elijah is considering buying a different set of tables and chairs. He reasons that the equation for the total cost (\$) (T) of buying a table and n chairs is: $T = 749 + 199n$

How much does a single chair cost?

______

b Use the equation to calculate the cost of the table and eight chairs.

______

ISBN: 9780170447492

Finding the sequence from the rule

- We can use the rule to find the sequence.

Examples:

1 Rule: $T = 2n + 1$

Term number (n)	1	2	3	4	5
Calculations	$T = 2 \times 1 + 1$				$T = 2 \times 5 + 1$
Value of term (T)	3	5	7	9	11

+ 2 + 2 + 2 + 2

1 What is the **first** term? $T = 2 \times 1 + 1 = 3$

2 What does the sequence go up by? **+2**

3 Check term 5. $T = 2 \times 5 + 1 = 11$ ✓

Tidy it up: 3, 5, 7, 9, 11

2 Rule: $T = 4n + 3$

Term number (n)	Calculations	Value of term (T)
1	$4 \times 1 + 3$	7
2		11
3		15
4		19
5	$4 \times 5 + 3$	23

+ 4 + 4 + 4 + 4

1 What is the **first** term? $T = 4 \times 1 + 3 = 7$

2 What does the sequence go up by? **+4**

3 Check term 5. $T = 2 \times 5 + 3 = 23$ ✓

Tidy it up: 7, 11, 15, 19, 23

 ISBN: 9780170447492

Calculate the first five terms of these sequences using the rule.

1 $T = 3n + 2$

Term number (n)	1	2	3	4	5
Calculations	3 x 1 + 2				
Value of term (V)					

Sequence: ______________________________

2 $T = 5n + 1$

Term number (n)	Calculations	Value of term (T)
1	5 x ____ + 1	
2		
3		
4		
5		

Sequence: ______________________________

3 $T = 2n + 6$

Term number (n)	1	2	3	4	5
Calculations					
Value of term (V)					

Sequence: ______________________________

4 $T = 6n + 3$

Term number (n)	1	2	3	4	5
Calculations					
Value of term (V)					

Sequence: ______________________________

5 $T = 4n + 1$

Term number (n)	1	2	3	4	5
Calculations					
Value of term (V)					

Sequence: ______________________________

6 $T = 5n + 4$

Term number (n)	1	2	3	4	5
Calculations					
Value of term (V)					

Sequence: ______________________________

7 $T = 7n + 10$

Term number (n)	1	2	3	4	5
Calculations					
Value of term (V)					

Sequence: ______________________________

ISBN: 9780170447492

Cross-number

The answers to the clues below are the first terms of a sequence.

1			2		3	15		4
		5				6		
7					8			
		17						
9			10		11			12
		13						
14					15			

Across		Down	
1	$n + 2$	**1**	$2n + 1$
3	$3n + 9$	**2**	$4n + 2$
5	$n + 12$	**3**	$2n + 10$
7	$3n + 6$	**4**	$2n + 19$
8	$3n + 15$	**5**	$2n + 11$
9	$3n + 10$	**6**	$4n + 13$
11	$n + 27$	**9**	$4n + 9$
13	$3n + 18$	**10**	$2n + 20$
14	$n + 24$	**11**	$2n + 26$
15	$n + 33$	**12**	$2n + 29$

ISBN: 9780170447492

Challenge 4

1 Find and highlight the 14 sequences in this number grid. The sequences may be horizontal or vertical, and each sequences is five terms long.

2	1	2	4	6	8	10	11	12	13
6	9	12	15	18	11	14	15	16	23
8	14	1	6	9	14	17	20	23	25
1	3	6	8	12	17	21	25	29	33
3	7	11	15	19	20	25	30	32	34
5	9	16	20	21	22	25	35	36	35
7	11	21	23	25	27	29	36	37	36
9	15	20	26	31	32	33	34	35	37
12	14	25	29	33	37	41	43	44	42
15	22	27	32	33	42	43	40	45	47

2 Fill in the gaps so that you complete sequences like those you have studied.

a 22, ________, 28, 31, ________, ________, 40

b 46, ________, ________, 58, ________, ________, 70

c −13, ________, −1, ________, ________, 17

d ________, ________, 37, ________, ________, 52

e −10, ________, ________, −1, ________, ________,

 ISBN: 9780170447492

Graphs

Plotting points

Positive coordinates

- A positive **x** coordinate tells you how far to move to the **right**.
- A positive **y** coordinate tells you how far to move **up**.
- Coordinates are written in brackets, and in **alphabetical order**: **(x, y)**.
- We use the word 'ax**i**s' for one axis, and the word 'ax**e**s' for more than one.

Consider the point **A** on the graph: it would be written as **(2, 3)**.

The **x** coordinate tells us how far to move to the **right**.

The **y** coordinate tells us how far to move **up**.

Start counting from the **origin (0, 0)**.

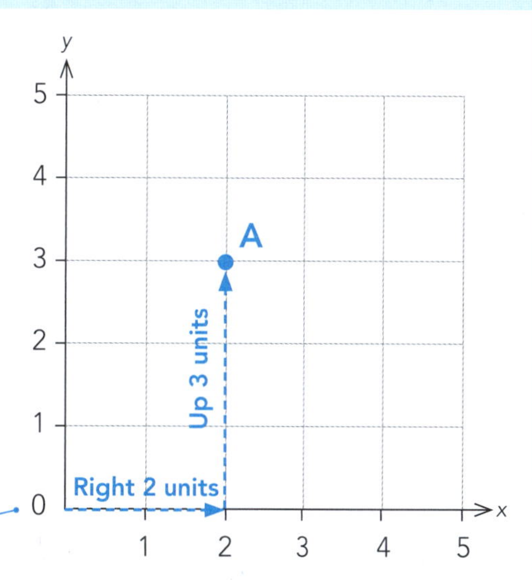

Sometimes not all the numbers are put on the axes.

Examples:

Only the **even** numbers are on these axes. Point **B** is at **(7, 5)**.

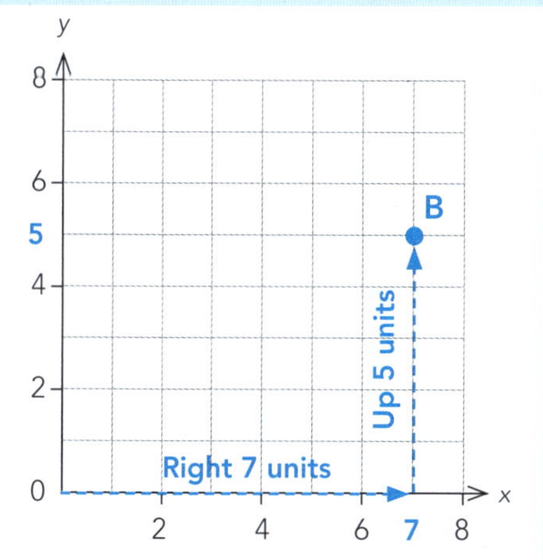

Only **multiples of 5** are on these axes. Point **C** is at **(4, 6)**.

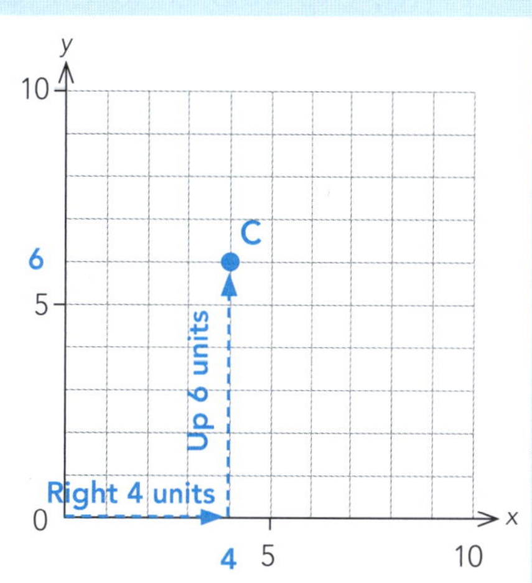

ISBN: 9780170447492

1 **a** Add the missing numbers to these axes.

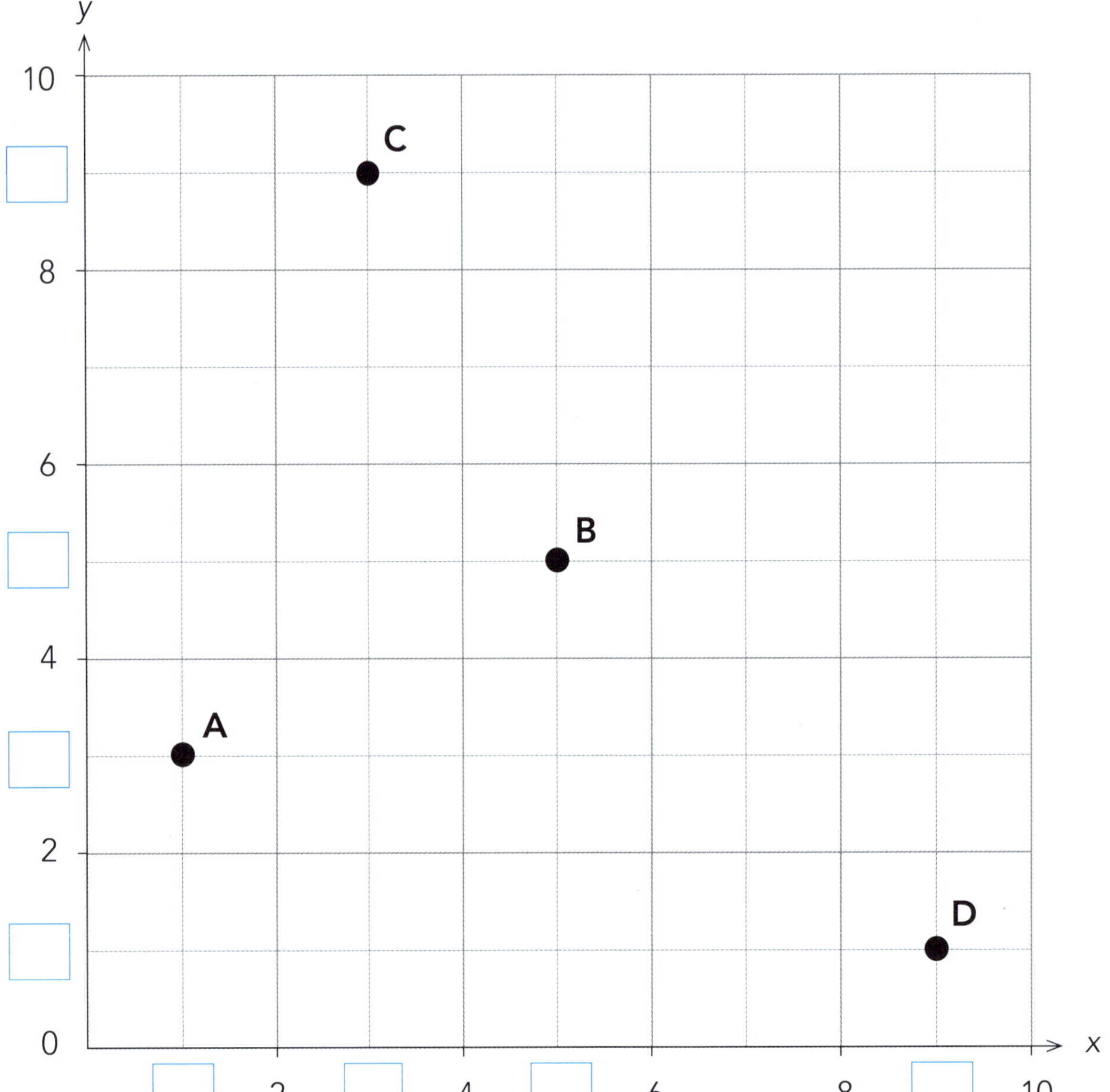

b Write the coordinates for the points A to D.

A (______, ______) B (______, ______)

C (______, ______) D (______, ______)

c Plot and label these points on the axes.

E (2,7) F (9, 9) J (5, 1) K (7, 5)

ISBN: 9780170447492

2 **a** Add the missing numbers to these axes.

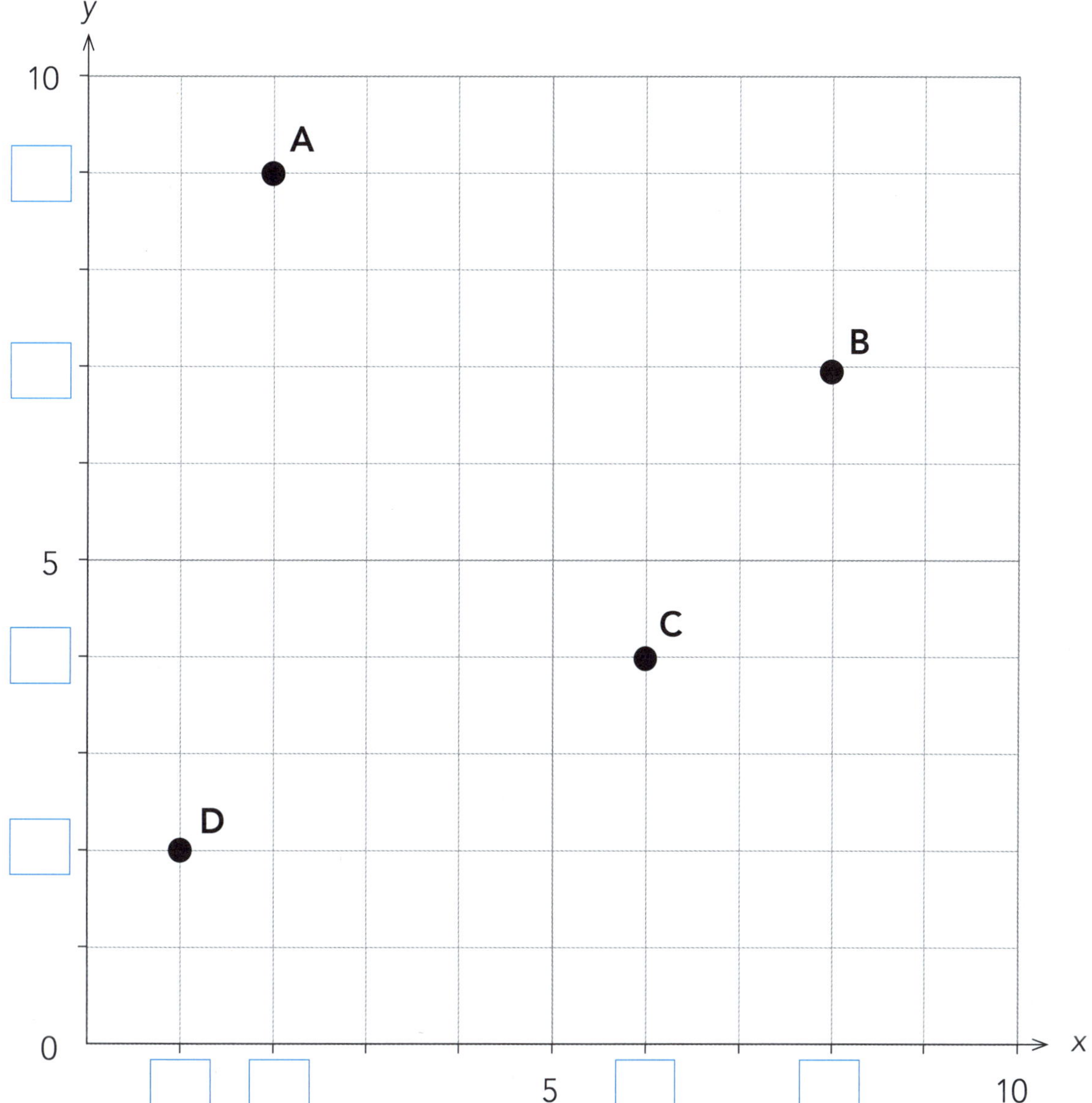

b Write the coordinates for the points A to D.

A (______, ______) B (______, ______)

C (______, ______) D (______, ______)

c Plot and label these points on the axes.

E (5,7) F (6, 10) J (2, 4) K (9, 3)

ISBN: 9780170447492

Zero coordinates

- If a coordinate falls on an axis, then that coordinate will be 0.

Examples:

A (0, 2)

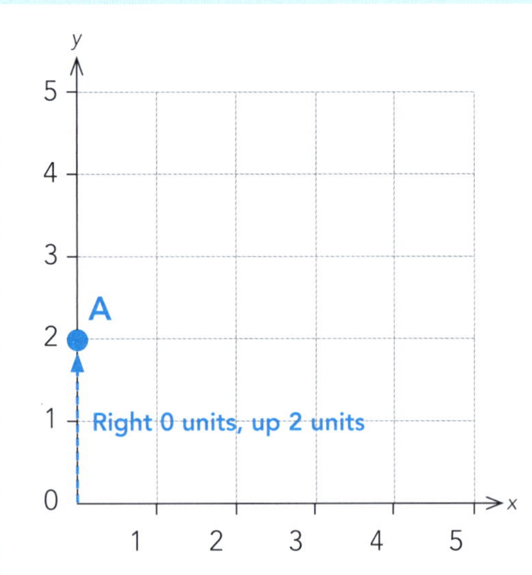

B (4, 0)

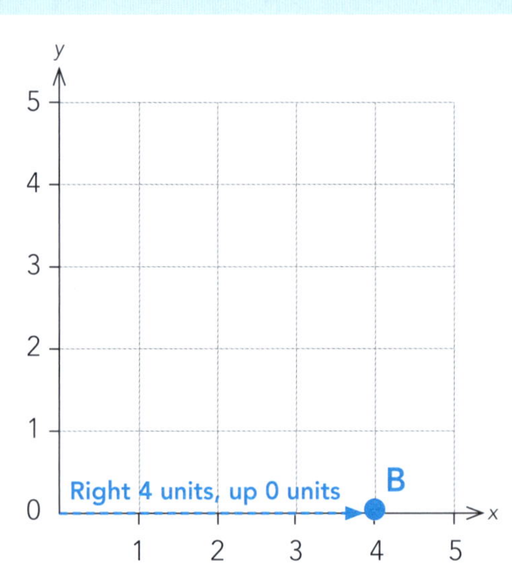

1 Write the coordinates for the points C and D.

C (______, ______)

D (______, ______)

2 Plot and label these points on the axes.

E (0, 4)

F (1, 0)

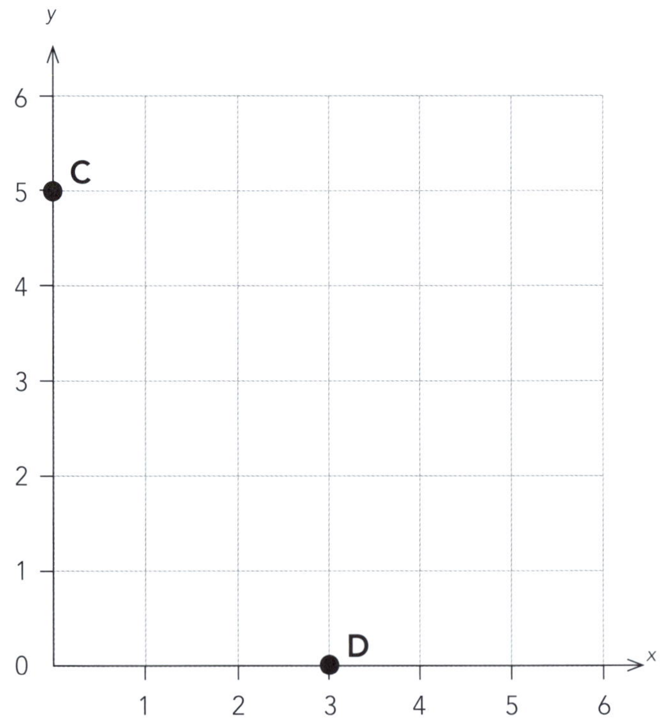

ISBN: 9780170447492

Putting it together

Write down the coordinates of the lettered points shown below.

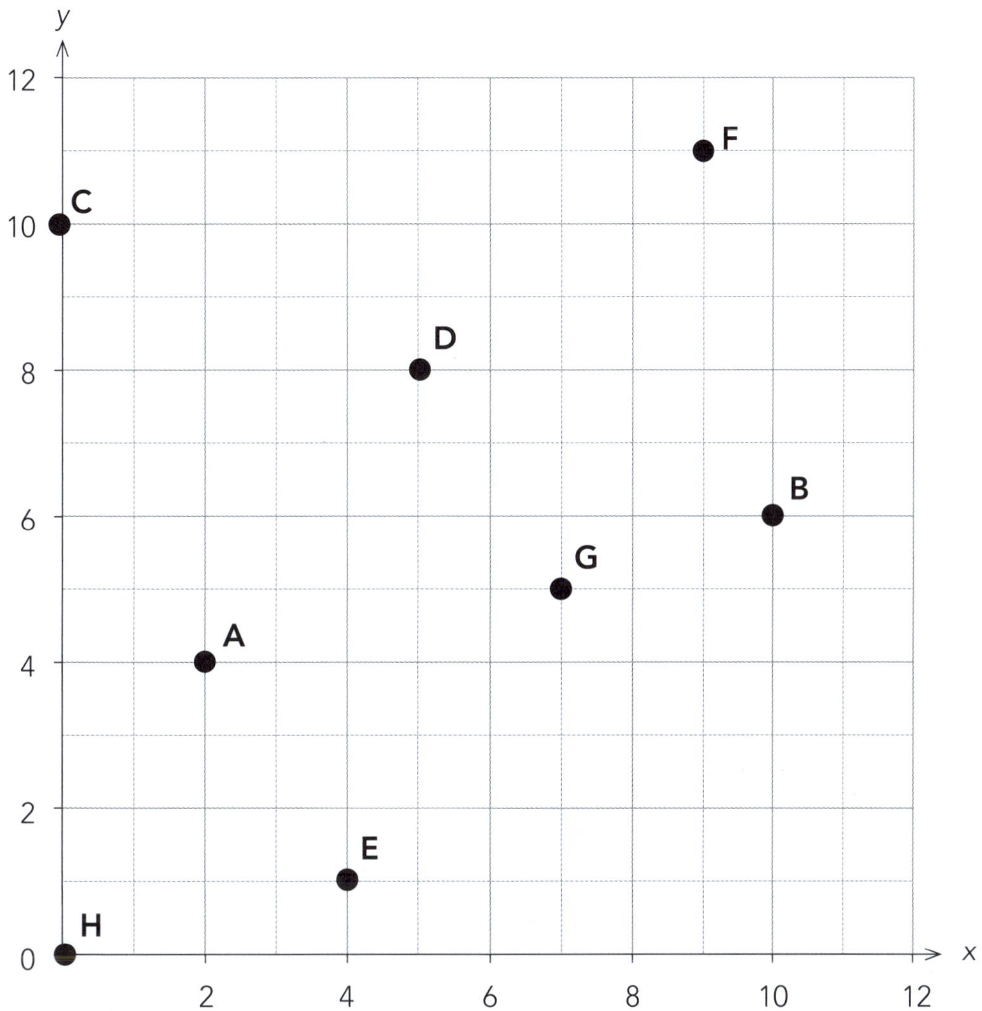

A (2, ____)

B (____, 6)

C (____, ____)

D (____, ____)

E (____, ____)

F (____, ____)

G (____, ____)

H (____, ____)

Plot these points on the axis.

I (10, 2)

J (1, 7)

K (6, 11)

L (3, 9)

M (0, 5)

N (9, 0)

ISBN: 9780170447492

Plotting a pattern on a graph

- You need to be able to continue a pattern, find the rule, and use it to plot the points on a graph.

Example:

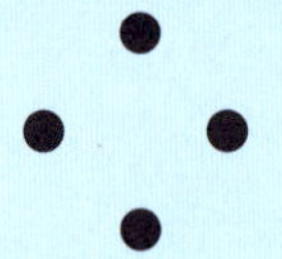
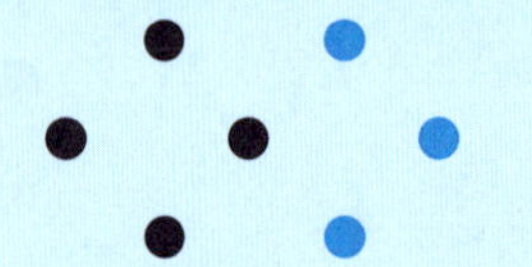
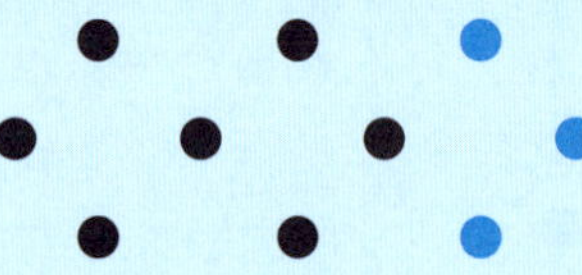

a Put the pattern in a table:

Number (n)	Value of term (V)	Coordinates
0	1	(0, 1)
1	4	(1, 4)
2	7	(2, 7)
3	10	(3, 10)
4	13	(4, 13)
5	16	(5, 16)

(Differences between successive values: − 3, + 3, + 3, + 3, + 3)

b Find the rule: V = 3 x pattern number + 1

c Tidy it up: $V = 3n + 1$

d Plot the points that fit on the graph:

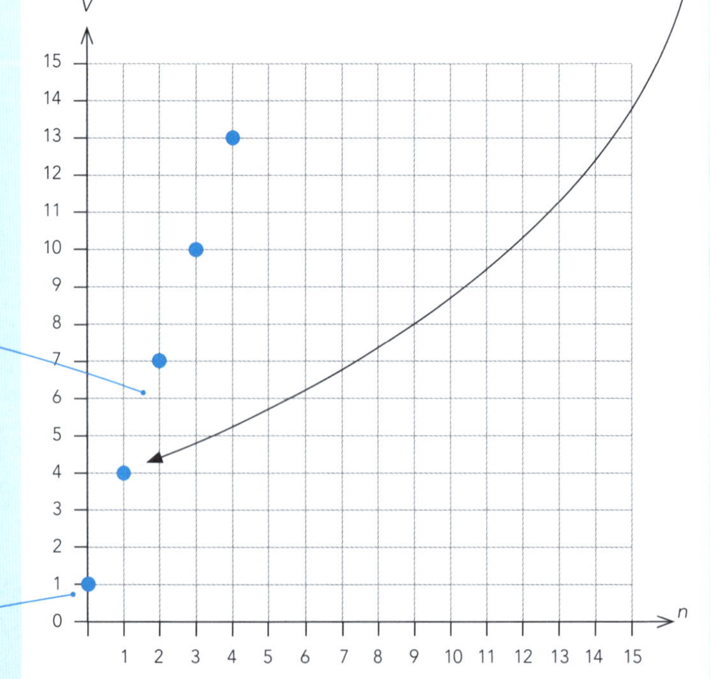

Notice the dots should be in a **straight line**, but don't draw a line through them.

$V = 3n + 1$
Notice that there is a point at **+ 1** on the vertical axis.

ISBN: 9780170447492

Complete the table, find the rule and plot the points on a graph.

1

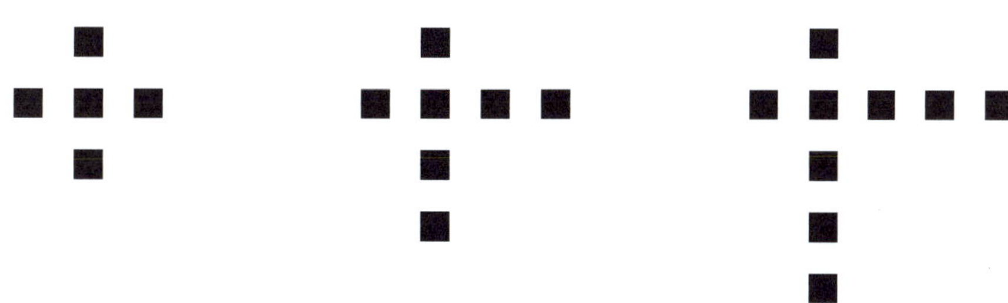

Number (n)	Value of term (V)	Coordinates
0		
1	5	(1, 5)
2		
3		
4		
5		
6		

Find the rule: $V =$ ______ x pattern number + ______

Tidy it up: $V =$ ______$n +$ ______

Plot the points:

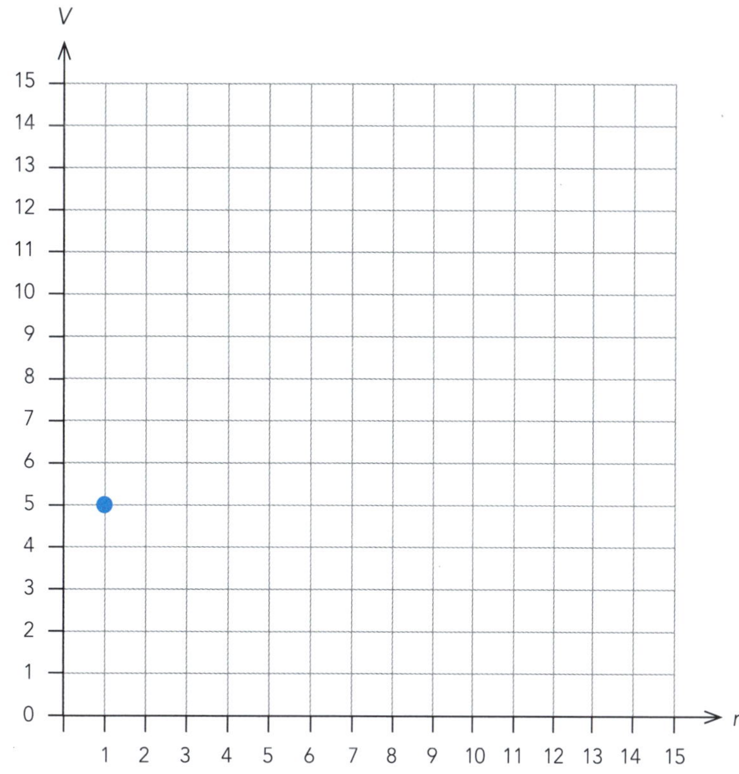

ISBN: 9780170447492

2

```
    ×              ×               ×
  × × ×        × × × ×       × × × × ×
    ×              ×               ×
```

Number (n)	Value of term (V)	Coordinates
0		
1	5	(1, 5)
2		
3		
4		
5		
6		

Find the rule: V = ______ x pattern number + ______

Tidy it up: V = ______ n + ______

Plot the points:

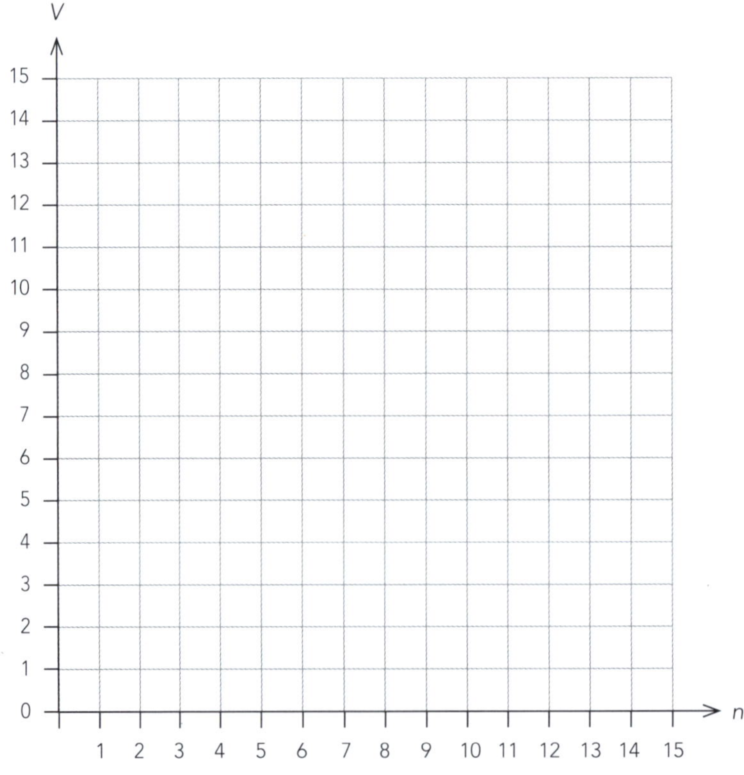

 ISBN: 9780170447492

3

Number (n)	Value of term (V)	Coordinates
0		
1		
2		
3		
4		
5		
6		

Find the rule: V = ______ x pattern number + ______

Tidy it up: V = ______n + ______

Plot the points:

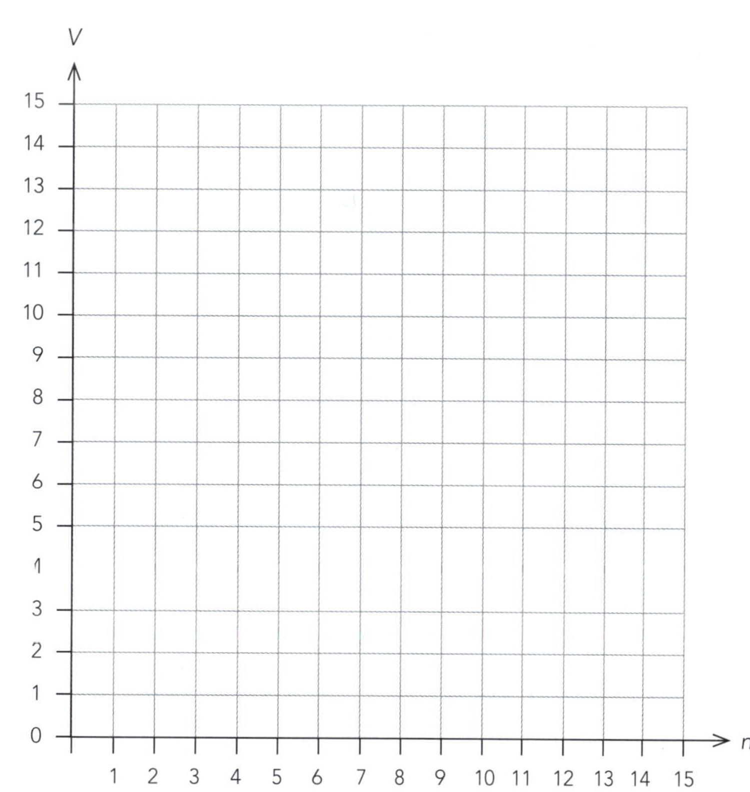

ISBN: 9780170447492

4

Number (n)	Value of term (V)	Coordinates
0		
1		
2		
3		
4		
5		
6		

Find the rule: $V =$ ______ x pattern number + ______

Tidy it up: $V =$ ______n + ______

Plot the points:

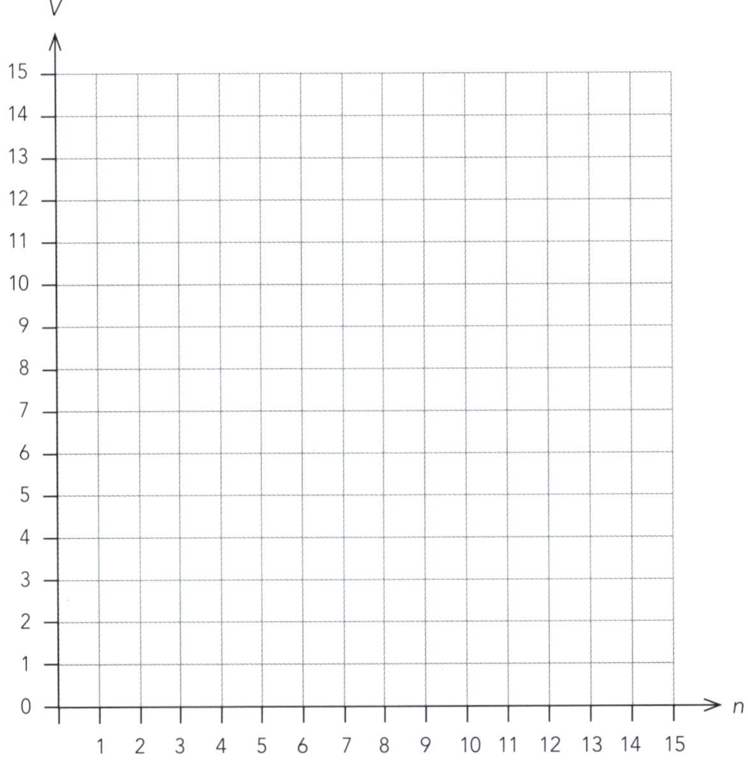

ISBN: 9780170447492

Revision 1

1 Rewrite these as expressions using symbols and the variable n.

a Four less than a number

= ______________________

b A quarter of a number

= ______________________

2 Simplify these expressions.

a $4p \times -2p =$ __________

b $\frac{12b}{3b} =$ __________

c $13a + 2a - a =$ __________

d $3c - 4d - 2c - d =$ __________

e $-2m \times 3mn =$ __________

f $18e \div 6 =$ __________

g $-g \times 2h \times -1 =$ __________

h $\frac{5}{15y} =$ __________

3 Let $a = 5$. Find the value of the following expressions.

a $5a + 7 =$ __________

= __________

b $\frac{50}{2a} =$ __________

= __________

c $2a^2 =$ __________

= __________

d $16 - 5a =$ __________

= __________

4 At the Fun Fair, every ride costs $8, and it costs $12 for admission. Let C represent the total cost for admission along with r rides.

a The variables are C, which stands for ______________________,

and ________, which stands for ______________________.

b They are called variables because ______________________.

c Write down the formula for calculating the total cost for admission and r rides.

$C =$ __________

d Calculate the total cost of admission and seven rides. $C =$ __________

= __________

= $__________

ISBN: 9780170447492

5 Solve the following equations.

a $a + 9 = 7$

b $\frac{b}{4} = 12$

c $-7c = 35$

d $d - 9 = -4$

e $-36 = -9e$

f $-3 = \frac{-f}{6}$

6 Write an equation for each of the following, and then solve it to find the mystery number. Use the variable n to represent the number.

a A number reduced by five is twenty.

b Triple a number comes to twenty-four.

7 Write the most appropriate instruction (**Simplify**, **Evaluate** or **Solve**) for each question. Then follow your chosen instruction in order to answer the question.

	Question	Instruction	Answer
a	$5a - 2b - 4 + b$		
b	$2d^2$ if $d = 3$		

 ISBN: 9780170447492

8 Draw the next shape in this pattern.

a 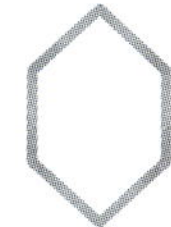 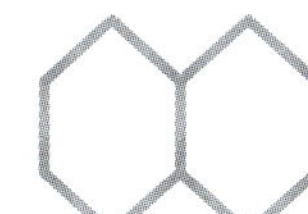 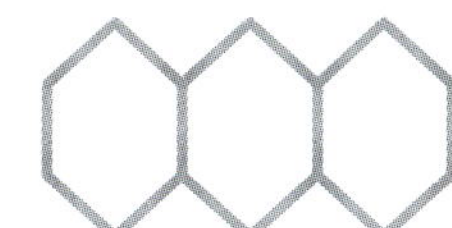

b Complete the table.

Term number (n)	0	1	2	3	4	5	6
Number of popsicle sticks (P)							

c The first term has ______ sticks and then I added ______ each time.

d Find the rule.

Number of popsicle sticks = ______ x term number + ______

P = __________

e Plot the points that fit on the graph.

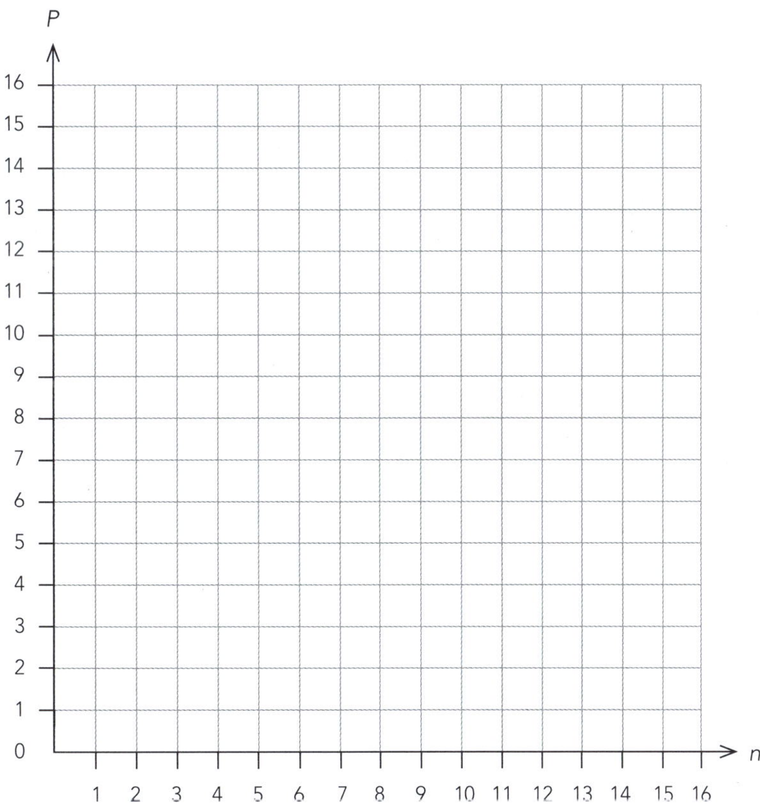

f How many popsicle sticks would be needed for the 50th shape?

P = ______________

= ________

ISBN: 9780170447492

9 Complete the table and find the rule for multiples of four that are bigger than fifteen.

Rule:

$V =$ ______

Term number (n)	1	2	3	4	5
Value of term (V)					

10 **a** For the sequence 19, 25, 31, 37, 43, …

a Find the rule.

Rule: ______

b The 15th term = ______

= ______

11 Use the rule to calculate the first five terms of this sequence:

$$V = 3n - 10$$

Term number (n)	1	2	3	4
Calculations				
Value of term (V)				

The next two terms of this sequence are: ______

12 **a** For his little brother's birthday, Tama and his family are buying a mat that has roads, a police station, a fire station, etc. on it, plus some Matchbox cars. The rule for the total cost ($) ($T$) of buying a mat and n cars is: $T = 3.49n + 5.99$

How much does a single car cost?

______

b Use the equation to calculate the cost of the mat and six cars.

______

______

______

13 Carter is buying a serving bowl ($15.99) and some small bowls ($6.99 each) for his flat.

Write the rule for the cost of a serving bowl plus n small bowls.

$T =$ ______

 ISBN: 9780170447492

Revision 2

1 Rewrite these as expressions using symbols and the variable n.

a Double a number

= ______________________

b A number times itself

= ______________________

2 Simplify these expressions.

a $p \times 2p \times -p =$ __________

b $\frac{15b}{3} =$ __________

c $a - 7a + 3a =$ __________

d $20 \div 5c =$ __________

e $\frac{18y}{2y} =$ __________

f $5ab \times 2b \times -3 =$ __________

g $2c - 4d + d - c + 9 =$ _______

h $p^2 + p =$ __________

3 Let $a = 4$. Find the value of the following expressions.

a $3a - 7 =$ ______________

= ______________

b $\frac{36}{-a} =$ ______________

= ______________

c $\frac{3a}{4} =$ ______________

= ______________

d $7a - a^2 =$ ______________

= ______________

4 Arlo is fencing an area for his six sheep. He needs a gate, which costs \$70, and posts, which cost \$14 each. Let C represent the total cost for a gate and p posts.

a The variables are C, which stands for ______________________________,

and _______, which stands for ______________________________________.

b They are called variables because ______________________________.

c Write down the formula for calculating the total cost for a gate and p posts.

$C =$ ______________

d Calculate the total cost of a gate and thirty posts. $C =$ ____________

= ____________

= \$____________

ISBN: 9780170447492

5 Solve the following equations.

a $a - 6 = 11$

b $\frac{b}{2} = 14$

c $9c = 45$

d $d + 11 = -2$

e $24 = -6e$

f $3 = \frac{-f}{8}$

6 Write an equation for each of the following, and then solve it to find the mystery number. Use the variable n to represent the number.

a Six more than a number is thirteen.

b Half a number comes to eighteen.

7 Write the most appropriate instruction (**Simplify**, **Evaluate** or **Solve**) for each question. Then follow your chosen instruction in order to answer the question.

	Question	Instruction	Answer
a	$60 = -12a$		
b	$7b - b^2 + 1 - b$		

 ISBN: 9780170447492

8 Draw the next shape in this pattern.

a

b Complete the table.

Term number (n)	0	1	2	3	4	5	6
Number of popsicle sticks (P)							

c The first term has ______ sticks and then I added ______ each time.

d Find the rule.

Number of popsicle sticks = ______ x pattern number + ______

P = __________

e Plot the points that fit on the graph.

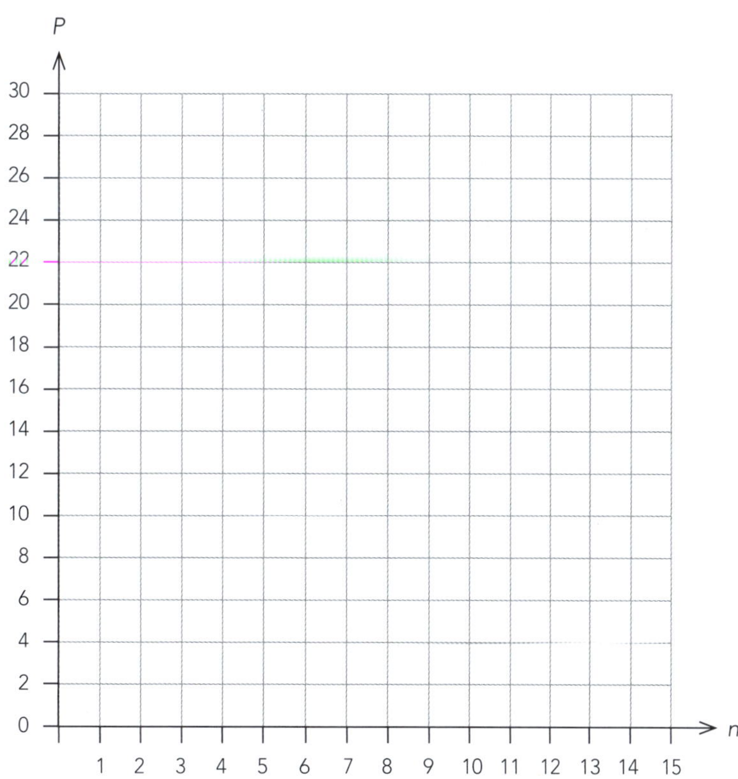

f How many popsicle sticks would be needed for the 50th shape?

P = ________________

= ______

ISBN: 9780170447492

9 Complete the table and find the rule: start at 11 and go up in threes.

Rule:

$V =$ ____________

Term number (n)	1	2	3	4	5
Value of term (V)					

10 For the sequence 10, 17, 24, 31, 38, …

a Find the rule.

Rule: ____________

b The 25th term = ____________

= ____________

11 Use the rule to calculate the first five terms of this sequence:

$$V = 15n + 10$$

Term number (n)	1	2	3	4
Calculations				
Value of term (V)				

The next two terms of this sequence are: ____________

12 **a** Mia has saved up for some fishing gear. She can buy a spinning rod and some lures. The rule for the total cost (\$) (T) of buying a rod and n lures is:
$T = 6.99n + 24.99$.

How much does the rod cost?

____

b Use the equation to calculate the cost of the rod and five lures.

____

____

____

13 Nikau is planting a garden bed with a kowhai tree (\$11.99) surrounded by tussocks (\$1.99 each).
Write the rule for the cost of a kowhai tree plus v tussocks.

$T =$ ____________

 ISBN: 9780170447492

Answers

Revision (pp. 6–9)

Working with integers (pp. 6–9)

Multiplying and dividing integers (p. 6)

1 18 **2** –10
3 12 **4** –5
5 –4 **6** 3
7 –24 **8** 5
9 –12 **10** 30
11 1 **12** –24
13 –4 **14** –30

Adding and subtracting integers (pp. 7–8)

1 4 **2** –5
3 –5 **4** –2
5 4 **6** –1
7 2
8 1 **9** –5
10 –9 **11** –11
12 7 **13** –3
14 4 **15** –2
16 –2 **17** 1
18 –5 **19** 0

Order of operations (p. 9)

B	Bracket
E	Exponents
D	Division
M	Multiplication
A	Addition
S	Subtraction

1 14 **2** 1
3 0 **4** 20
5 3 **6** 8
7 20 **8** 3
9 2 **10** 13
11 2 **12** 0
13 8 **14** 28

The language of algebra (pp. 10–16)

From words to expressions (p. 10)

1. add, more, plus, sum, total, increase by
2. multiply, times, lots of, product
3. subtract, minus, less than, takeaway, decrease by
4. divide, goes into, division, split

5 $n + 5$ **6** $n - 6$
7 $3n$ or $3 \times n$ **8** $n \div 8$
9 $7 - n$ **10** $n + 20$
11 $2n$ or $2 \times n$ **12** $n - 10$
13 $n - 4$ **14** $9n$ or $9 \times n$

Finding the value of a symbol (pp. 11–12)

1 2 **2** 5
3 6 **4** 5
5 4 **6** 2
7 3 **8** 3
9 ✹ = 5
☆ = 3
❆ = 6
❁ = 4
ஐ = 2
10 $a = 5$ **11** $b = 9$
12 $c = 10$ **13** $d = 6$
14 $e = 6$ **15** $f = 6$
16 $f = 3$ **17** $g = 2$
18 $h = 24$ **19** $i = 5$
20 $j = 7$ **21** $k = 8$
22 $m = 4$ **23** $n = 3$
24 $p = 2$ **25** $q = 11$
26 $r = 4$ **27** $s = 16$
28 $t = 5$ **29** $u = 5$

Phrases to expressions (pp. 13–15)

	Phrase	Expression
1	Twice *e*	$2e$
2	*e* reduced by two	$e - 2$
3	A total of *e* and *f*	$e + f$
4	*e* shared between two	$\frac{e}{2}$
5	Two more than *e*	$e + 2$
6	2 decreased by *f*	$2 - f$
7	Half of *f*	$\frac{f}{2}$
8	*f* increased by two	$f + 2$
9	*f* subtracted from *e*	$e - f$
10	*e* lots of *f*	ef
11	2 split between *e*	$2 \div e$
12	The number of *f*s that go into *e*	$\frac{e}{f}$

ISBN: 9780170447492

	Phrase	Expression
13	Two divided by *f*	$\frac{2}{f}$
14	2 less than *f*	$f - 2$
15	Twice *f*	$2f$
16	*f* and *e*	$f + e$
17	Double *f*	$2f$
18	The sum of *e* and 2	$e + 2$

Your answers may be different from those below. If so, check with your teacher.

19 $y + 2$ **20** $4y$
21 $\frac{y}{9}$ or $y \div 9$ **22** $2 - y$
23 $\frac{y}{2}$ or $y \div 2$ **24** $y - 1$
25 $y - 5$ **26** $\frac{10}{y}$ or $10 \div y$

Questions **27–34**: some examples of correct answers are:

27 Six with *a* added to it.
28 Seven with *b* subtracted from it.
29 Six times *c*. **30** Half of *d*.
31 Two less than *e*. **32** Eight divided by *f*.
33 Nine times *g*. **34** Three more than *h*.

More about variables (p. 16)

1 **a** The variable is *h* and it stands for the number of hours worked.
b Total = $12h$
= 12×4
= \$48

2 **a** The variable is *c* and it stands for the number of cousins that can come.
b Total friends = $10 - c - 1$
= $10 - 3 - 1$
= 6

Simplifying expressions (pp. 17–25)

Multiplying (pp. 17–18)

1 $5a$ **2** b^3
3 $3cd$ **4** $8e$
5 $6fg$ **6** $12h^2$
7 $-4j$ **8** $-k^2$
9 $2b$ **10** cp
11 $8d$ **12** $2be$
13 f^2 **14** $4gs$
15 $3h^2$ **16** $-3gh$
17 $-8n$ **18** $10p$
19 $24m^2$ **20** n^2t
21 s^2u^2 **22** $7v^2$
23 $-18p^3$ **24** $-2q^2z$

25

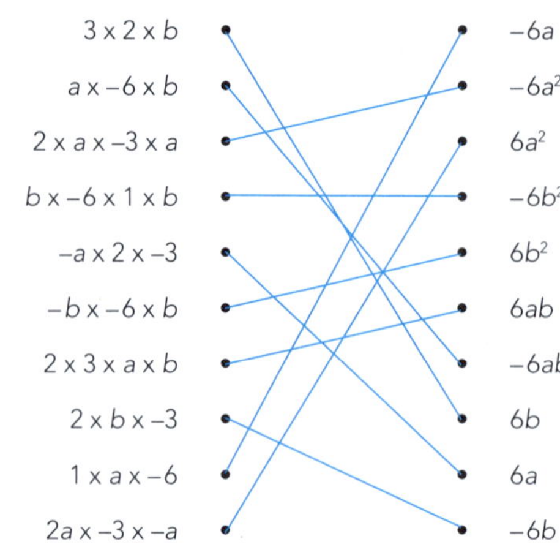

Dividing (pp. 19–20)

1 $\frac{b}{4}$ **2** $\frac{5}{p}$
3 $4a$ **4** $\frac{1}{3d}$
5 $\frac{y}{2}$ **6** $2d$
7 $\frac{10}{e}$ **8** $12b$
9 b **10** $\frac{g}{3}$
11 $\frac{1}{5p}$ **12** 3
13 $6m$ **14** $\frac{1}{8a}$
15 1 **16** 8
17 $\frac{8}{v}$ **18** $-3b$
19

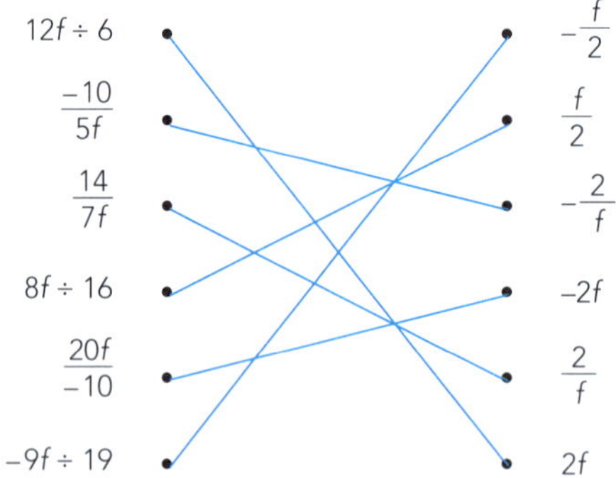

Putting it together (p. 21)

1 $2d$ **2** $2de$
3 $2e$ **4** $6e$
5 $\frac{2}{d}$ **6** 2
7 1 **8** $\frac{d}{2}$
9 6 **10** $-6d$
11 $-e$ **12** $-d$
13 $-2d$ **14** d^2
15 d **16** $-6e$

ISBN: 9780170447492

Like terms (p. 22)

1 Unlike
2 Like
3 Unlike
4 Like
5 Like
6 Unlike
7 Like
8 Unlike
9 Like
10 Like
11 Unlike
12 Unlike
13 Unlike
14 Like
15 (2p), p^2, 2, (–p), (10p), q, (p), pq

Adding and subtracting (pp. 23–24)

A

1 $2a$
2 $4t$
3 $5y$
4 $5d$
5 $8a$
6 $5b$
7 5
8 $6b$
9 $2f$
10 –4
11 $8y$
12 $5p$
13 $-e$
14 $3c$

B

1 $2p$
2 $9a$
3 $9a + 4$
4 $8b + c$
5 $9a$
6 f
7 $6a - 2$
8 $5y$
9 $2b$
10 $4a - 3b$

C

1 $2a$
2 $3x$
3 $9a$
4 $8y$
5 $8a + 2b$
6 $2y + 6$
7 $x + 4$
8 $3a + 3b$
9 $3x + 5y$
10 $p + 5q$
11 $6a + 5b + 4$
12 $9y + 5 - x$
13 $3f - 4g$
14 $4x - 3y$

Mixing it up (p. 25)

		✓/✗	Correct solution
1	$p \times p \times 2 = 2p$	✗	$p \times p \times 2 = 2p^2$
2	$\frac{12pq}{4} = 3pq$	✓	
3	$a + a^2 + a = a^2 + 2a$	✓	
4	$2t \times 5t = 10t$	✗	$2t \times 5t = 10t^2$
5	$6a + a - 2 - a + 7 = 6a + 9$	✗	$6a + a - 2 - a + 7 = 6a + 5$
6	$10m \div 2m = 5m$	✗	$10m \div 2m = 5$
7	$15f + 2g - 10f - g = 5f - g$	✗	$15f + 2g - 10f - g = 5f + g$
8	$-24 \div 8c = \frac{-3}{c}$	✓	

Challenge 1 (p. 26)

1

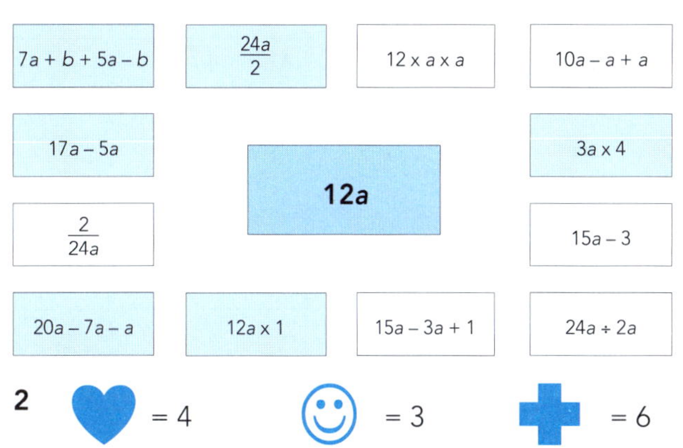

2 = 4 = 3 = 6

Formulae and substitution (pp. 27–30)

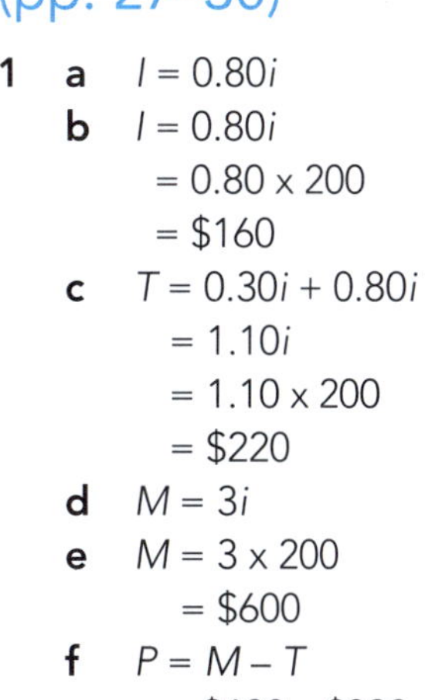

1 a $I = 0.80i$

b $I = 0.80i$
$= 0.80 \times 200$
$= \$160$

c $T = 0.30i + 0.80i$
$= 1.10i$
$= 1.10 \times 200$
$= \$220$

d $M = 3i$

e $M = 3 \times 200$
$= \$600$

f $P = M - T$
$= \$600 - \$220$
$= \$380$

2 a $A = 15h$
$= 15 \times 6$
$= \$90$

b $A = 12h$

c Fruit-picking earns $15 \times 3 = \$45$
Gardening earns $12 \times 4 = \$48$
Gardening earns more money by $3.

d Her grandmother pays her $14 per hour plus $10 each time she comes.

e $A = 13h + 7$

3 a $C = 20 + 2k$

b $C = 20 + 2k$
$= 20 + 2 \times 9$
$= \$38$

4

Formula	$b = 1$	$b = 2$	$b = 5$	$b = 10$
$A = 3b$	$A = 3b$ $= 3 \times 1$ $= 3$	$A = 3b$ $= 3 \times 2$ $= 6$	$A = 3b$ $= 3 \times 5$ $= 15$	$A = 3b$ $= 3 \times 10$ $= 30$
$A = b + 7$	$A = b + 7$ $= 1 + 7$ $= 8$	$A = b + 7$ $= 2 + 7$ $= 9$	$A = b + 7$ $= 5 + 7$ $= 12$	$A = b + 7$ $= 10 + 7$ $= 17$

ISBN: 9780170447492

Formula	$b = 1$	$b = 2$	$b = 5$	$b = 10$
$A = 20 - b$	$A = 20 - b$ $= 20 - 1$ $= 19$	$A = 20 - b$ $= 20 - 2$ $= 18$	$A = 20 - b$ $= 20 - 5$ $= 15$	$A = 20 - b$ $= 20 - 10$ $= 10$
$A = b - 4$	$A = b - 4$ $= 1 - 4$ $= -3$	$A = b - 4$ $= 2 - 4$ $= -2$	$A = b - 4$ $= 5 - 4$ $= 1$	$A = b - 4$ $= 10 - 4$ $= 6$
$A = \frac{20}{b}$	$A = \frac{20}{b}$ $= \frac{20}{1}$ $= 20$	$A = \frac{20}{b}$ $= \frac{20}{2}$ $= 10$	$A = \frac{20}{b}$ $= \frac{20}{5}$ $= 4$	$A = \frac{20}{b}$ $= \frac{20}{10}$ $= 2$
$A = b^2$	$A = b^2$ $= 1 \times 1$ $= 1$	$A = b^2$ $= 2 \times 2$ $= 4$	$A = b^2$ $= 5 \times 5$ $= 25$	$A = b^2$ $= 10 \times 10$ $= 100$
$A = 5 - 2b$	$A = 5 - 2b$ $= 5 - 2 \times 1$ $= 3$	$A = 5 - 2b$ $= 5 - 2 \times 2$ $= 1$	$A = 5 - 2b$ $= 5 - 2 \times 5$ $= -5$	$A = 5 - 2b$ $= 5 - 2 \times 10$ $= -15$

Challenge 2 (p. 31)

	[1] 1	[2] 2		[3] 3	6	
[4] 2		4		4		[5] 1
[6] 1	1		[7] 1		[8] 5	3
		[9] 1	4	4		
[10] 7	2		4		[11] 8	[12] 6
0		[13] 2		[14] 3		0
	[15] 1	9		[16] 6	8	

Solving equations (pp. 32–40)

Adding and subtracting (pp. 32–35)

1 $a + 4 = 10$
$a + 4 - 4 = 10 - 4$
$a = 6$
Check: $6 + 4 = 10$ ✓

2 $b - 7 = 12$
$b - 7 + 7 = 12 + 7$
$b = 19$
Check: $19 - 7 = 12$ ✓

3 $c - 6 = 20$
$c - 6 + 6 = 20 + 6$
$c = 26$
Check: $26 - 6 = 20$ ✓

4 $d + 9 = 13$
$d + 9 - 9 = 13 - 9$
$d = 4$
Check: $4 + 9 = 13$ ✓

5 $e - 11 = 22$
$e - 11 + 11 = 22 + 11$
$e = 33$
Check: $33 - 11 = 22$ ✓

6 $f - 5 = 0$
$f - 5 + 5 = 0 + 5$
$f = 5$
Check: $5 - 5 = 0$ ✓

7 $g + 15 = 18$
$g + 15 - 15 = 18 - 15$
$g = 3$
Check: $3 + 15 = 18$ ✓

8 $h + 6 = 2$
$h + 6 - 6 = 2 - 6$
$h = -4$
Check: $-4 + 6 = 2$ ✓

9 $i + 12 = 0$
$i + 12 - 12 = 0 - 12$
$i = -12$
Check: $-12 + 12 = 0$ ✓

10 $j - 1 = -9$
$j - 1 + 1 = -9 + 1$
$j = -8$
Check: $-8 - 1 = -9$ ✓

11 $v = 14$ **12** $s = 4$
13 $p = 14$ **14** $t = -1$
15 $u = -35$ **16** $w = -11$
17 $a = 15$ **18** $b = -19$
19 $z = 2$ **20** $q = -3$
21 $r = 18$ **22** $k = 10$
23 $n = 16$ **24** $m = 16$
25 $d = -57$ **26** $g = -4$
27 $y = 23$ **26** $w = -18$

Find the errors (p. 36)

1	$p + 7 = 2$ $p + 7 - 7 = 2 - 7$ $p = -5$	✗
2	$h - 8 = 2$ $h - 8 + 8 = 2 + 8$ $h = 10$	✓
3	$z - 9 = -4$ $z - 9 + 9 = -4 + 9$ $z = 5$	✗
4	$w + 13 = -6$ $w + 13 - 13 = -6 - 13$ $w = -19$	✗
5	$8 - v = 3$ $8 - v - 8 = 3 - 8$ $-v = -5$ $v = 5$	✓
6	$19 = -12 - w$ $19 + 12 = -w$ $31 = -w$ $w = -31$	✓

ISBN: 9780170447492

Multiplying and dividing (pp. 37–39)

1 $\frac{a}{2} = 7$

$\frac{2}{1} \times \frac{a}{2} = 7 \times 2$

$a = 14$

Check: $\frac{14}{2} = 7$ ✓

2 $3 \times b = 18$

$\frac{3 \times b}{3} = \frac{18}{3}$

$b = 6$

Check: $3 \times 8 = 18$ ✓

3 $8c = 24$

$\frac{8c}{8} = \frac{24}{8}$

$c = 3$

Check: $8 \times 3 = 24$ ✓

4 $\frac{d}{5} = 20$

$\frac{5}{1} \times \frac{d}{5} = 20 \times 5$

$d = 100$

Check: $\frac{100}{5} = 20$ ✓

5 $7e = 42$

$\frac{7e}{7} = \frac{42}{7}$

$e = 6$

Check: $7 \times 6 = 42$ ✓

6 $\frac{f}{9} = 3$

$\frac{9}{1} \times \frac{f}{9} = 3 \times 9$

$f = 27$

Check: $\frac{27}{9} = 3$ ✓

7 $\frac{g}{6} = -2$

$\frac{6}{1} \times \frac{g}{6} = -2 \times 6$

$g = -12$

Check: $\frac{-12}{6} = -2$ ✓

8 $4h = 32$

$\frac{4h}{4} = \frac{32}{4}$

$h = 8$

Check: $4 \times 8 = 32$ ✓

9 $5i = -35$

$\frac{5i}{5} = \frac{-35}{5}$

$i = -7$

Check: $5 \times -7 = -35$ ✓

10 $j \div 4 = 25$

$4 \times j \div 4 = 25 \times 4$

$j = 100$

Check: $100 \div 4 = 25$ ✓

11 $3k = 90$

$\frac{3k}{3} = \frac{90}{3}$

$k = 30$

Check: $3 \times 30 = 90$ ✓

12 $15m = -45$

$\frac{15m}{15} = \frac{-45}{15}$

$m = -3$

Check: $15 \times -3 = -45$ ✓

13 $\frac{n}{10} = -8$

$\frac{10}{1} \times \frac{n}{10} = -8 \times 10$

$n = -80$

Check: $\frac{-80}{10} = -8$ ✓

14 $p \div 11 = -5$

$11 \times p \div 11 = -5 \times 11$

$p = -55$

Check: $-55 \div 11 = -5$ ✓

15 $q = 120$ **16** $r = -2$
17 $s = -24$ **18** $t = 16$
19 $u = 36$ **20** $w = -14$

Mixing it up (p. 40)

1 $a = 26$ **2** $b = 32$
3 $c = 10$ **4** $d = -200$
5 $e = 42$ **6** $f = -49$
7 $g = -140$ **8** $h = -9$
9 $i = -12$ **10** $j = -80$

Challenge 3 (p. 41)

	[1] 2	[2] 1		[3] 3	1	
[4] 6		7		9		[5] 8
[6] 4	2		[7] 1		[8] 5	1
		[9] 1	0	0		
[10] 2	5		1		[11] 7	[12] 5
4		[13] 4		[14] 1		1
	[15] 2	9		[16] 6	0	

Forming then solving equations (pp. 42–43)

1
$3n = 18$
$\frac{3n}{3} = \frac{18}{3}$
$n = 6$

2
$\frac{n}{2} = 20$
$\frac{n}{2} \times \frac{2}{1} = 20 \times 2$
$n = 40$

3
$n + 10 = 17$
$n + 10 - 10 = 17 - 10$
$n = 7$

4
$n - 5 = 9$
$n - 5 + 9 = 9 + 5$
$n = 14$

5
$\frac{n}{2} = 12$
$\frac{n}{2} \times \frac{2}{1} = 12 \times 2$
$n = 24$

6
$6n = 12$
$6n \times \frac{1}{6} = 12 \times \frac{1}{6}$
$n = 2$

7
$2n = 16$
$2n \times \frac{1}{2} = 16 \times \frac{1}{2}$
$n = 8$

8
$\frac{n}{3} = 12$
$\frac{n}{3} \times \frac{3}{1} = 12 \times 3$
$n = 36$

9
$n - 3 = 9$
$n - 3 + 3 = 9 + 3$
$n = 12$

10
$n + 4 = 10$
$n + 4 - 4 = 10 - 4$
$n = 6$

11
$3 + 4 + n = 9$
$7 + n - 7 = 9 - 7$
$n = 2$

12
$\frac{n}{2} = 5$
$\frac{n}{2} \times \frac{2}{1} = 5 \times 2$
$n = 10$

13
$n - 5 = 8$
$n - 5 + 5 = 8 + 5$
$n = 13$

14
$3n = 15$
$3n \times \frac{1}{3} = 15 \times \frac{1}{3}$
$n = 5$

Understanding instructions in algebra (p. 44–45)

	Question	Instruction	Answer
1	$10 - a = 3$	Solve	$a = 7$
2	$p + t + 2p$	Simplify	$3p + t$
3	$8b \times 2b$	Simplify	$16b^2$
4	$\frac{12y}{4}$	Simplify	$3y$
5	$3x + 6 - x$	Simplify	$2x + 6$
6	$4x + 2$ when $x = 3$	Evaluate	14
7	$6d = -12$	Solve	$d = -2$
8	$\frac{10v^2}{v}$	Simplify	$10v$
9	$3h^2$ if $h = 2$	Evaluate	12
10	$\frac{g}{9} = -3$	Solve	$g = -27$

Patterns (pp. 46–76)

Continuing patterns (p. 47)

1

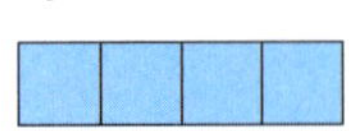

2

3

4

5

6

7

From pictures to numbers (p. 48)

1	2	4	6	8	10
2	4	7	10	13	
3	1	3	5	7	9
4	13	9	5	1	
5	21	17	13	9	

Describing patterns (pp. 49–50)

1. I started with 2 popsicle sticks and then I added 1 each time.
2. I started with 3 dots and then I added 2 each time.
3. I started with 2 crosses and then I added 2 each time.
4. I started with 4 diamonds and then I added 3 each time.
5. I started with 12 popsicle sticks and then I subtracted 2 each time.
6. I started with 16 dots and then I subtracted 3 each time.
7. I started with 25 diamonds and then I subtracted 5 each time.
8. I started with 10 crosses and then I subtracted 1 each time.

ISBN: 9780170447492

Patterns into tables (pp. 51–53)

1

Shape number	Number of diamonds
1	5
2	6
3	7
4	8
5	9
6	10

+ 1 + 1 + 1 + 1 + 1

2

Shape number	1	2	3	4	5	6
Number of crosses	1	4	7	10	13	16

+ 3 + 3 + 3

3

Shape number	Number of dots
1	5
2	7
3	9
4	11
5	13
6	15

+ 2

4

Shape number	1	2	3	4	5	6
Number of stars	1	5	9	13	17	21

+ 4

5

Shape number	Number of squares
1	8
2	7
3	6
4	5
5	4
6	3

− 1

6

Shape number	1	2	3	4	5	6
Number of stars	17	14	11	8	5	2

− 3

7

Shape number	Number of dots
1	25
2	21
3	17
4	13
5	9

Finding term 'zero' (pp. 54–56)

1

Term number	0	1	2	3	4	5	6
Number of stars	4	6	8	10	12	14	16

+ 2

2

Term number	Number of dots
0	4
1	7
2	10
3	13
4	16
5	19

3

Term number	0	1	2	3	4	5	6
Number of squares	5	7	9	11	13	15	17

4

Term number	0	1	2	3	4	5	6
Number of crosses	1	6	11	16	21	26	31

5

Term number	Number of diamonds
0	2
1	4
2	6
3	8
4	10
5	12

6

Term number	0	1	2	3	4	5	6
Number of triangles	2	6	10	14	18	22	26

ISBN: 9780170447492

7

Term number	Number of squares
0	3
1	9
2	15
3	21
4	27
5	33

Finding the rule from shapes and a table (pp. 57–63)

1

Term number (n)	Number of dots (D)
0	1
1	3
2	5
3	7
4	9
5	11

– 2
+ 2

In words: The first term has three dots and then I added two each time.
Find the mathematical rule:
Number of dots = 2 x term number + 1
Tidy it up: $D = 2n + 1$
Word rule: The number of dots is calculated by multiplying the term number by two and then adding one.
Use the rule: How many dots would be needed for the 20th shape?
$D = 2 \times 20 + 1$
$= 40 + 1$
$= 41$

2

Term number (n)	Number of squares (S)
0	2
1	5
2	8
3	11
4	14
5	17

+ 3

In words: The first term has five squares and then I added three each time.
Find the mathematical rule:
Number of squares = 3 x term number + 2
Tidy it up: $S = 3n + 2$
Word rule: The number of squares is calculated by multiplying the term number by three and then adding two.
Use the rule: How many squares would be needed for the 30th shape?
$S = 3 \times 30 + 2$
$= 90 + 2$
$= 92$

3

Term number (n)	Number of stars (S)
0	4
1	9
2	14
3	19
4	24
5	29

+ 5

In words: The first term has nine stars and then I added five each time.
Find the mathematical rule:
Number of stars = 5 x term number + 4
Tidy it up: $S = 5n + 4$
Word rule: The number of stars is calculated by multiplying the term number by five and then adding four.
Use the rule: How many stars would be needed for the 25th shape?
$S = 5 \times 25 + 4$
$= 125 + 4$
$= 129$

4

Term number (n)	Number of squares (S)
0	3
1	4
2	5
3	6
4	7
5	8

+ 1

In words: The first term has four squares and then I added one each time.
Find the mathematical rule:
Number of squares = 1 x term number + 3
Tidy it up: $S = 1n + 3$
Word rule: The number of squares is calculated by multiplying the term number by one and then adding three.

ISBN: 9780170447492

Use the rule: How many squares would be needed for the 35th shape?

$S = 1 \times 35 + 3$
$= 35 + 3$
$= 38$

5

Term number (n)	Number of crosses (C)
0	3
1	7
2	11
3	15
4	19
5	23

In words: The first term has seven crosses and then I added four each time.

Find the mathematical rule:

Number of crosses = 4 x term number + 3

Tidy it up: $C = 4n + 3$

Word rule: The number of crosses is calculated by multiplying the term number by four and then adding three.

Use the rule: How many crosses would be needed for the 50th shape?

$C = 4 \times 50 + 3$
$= 200 + 3$
$= 203$

Finding the rule from a description (pp. 64–67)

1

Term number (n)	Value of term (T)
0	2
1	5
2	8
3	11
4	14
5	17

+ 3

Rule: $T = 3n + 2$

2

Term number (n)	0	1	2	3	4	5
Value of term (T)	6	8	10	12	14	16

+ 2

Rule: $T = 2n + 6$

3

Term number (n)	Value of term (T)
0	5
1	10
2	15
3	20
4	25
5	30

+ 5

Rule: $T = 5n + 5$

4

Term number (n)	0	1	2	3	4	5
Value of term (T)	9	13	17	21	25	29

+ 4

Rule: $T = 4n + 9$

5

Term number (n)	Value of term (T)
0	9
1	12
2	15
3	18
4	21
5	24

+ 3

Rule: $T = 3n + 9$

6

Term number (n)	0	1	2	3	4	5
Value of term (T)	14	16	18	20	22	24

+ 2

Rule: $T = 2n + 14$

7

Term number (n)	Value of term (T)
0	0
1	3
2	6
3	9
4	12
5	15

Rule: $T = 3n + 0$
or $T = 3n$

ISBN: 9780170447492

8

Term number (n)	0	1	2	3	4	5
Value of term (T)	1	3	5	7	9	11

Rule: $T = 2n + 1$

9

Term number (n)	1	2	3	4
Value of term (T)	16	18	20	22

Rule: $T = 2n + 14$

10

Term number (n)	Value of term (T)
1	9
2	18
3	27
4	36
5	45

Rule: $T = 9n + 0$
or $T = 9n$

11

Term number (n)	1	2	3	4	5
Value of term (T)	100	110	120	130	140

Rule: $T = 10n + 90$

12

Term number (n)	Value of term (T)
1	12
2	24
3	36
4	48
5	60

Rule: $T = 12n + 0$
or $T = 12n$

Finding the rule from a list (pp. 68–69)

1 4, 5, 6, 7, 8, …
−1 +1
The first term has 5 and then I added 1 each time. Term zero will be 4.
Rule: $T = 1n + 4$ or $T = n + 4$

2 3, 6, 9, 12, 15, …
−3 +3
The first term has 6 and then I added 3 each time. Term zero will be 3.
Rule: $T = 3n + 3$

3 5, 9, 13, 17, 21, 25, …
−4 +4
The first term has 9 and then I added 4 each time. Term zero will be 5.
Rule: $T = 4n + 5$

4 9, 11, 13, 15, 17, …
−4 +4
The first term has 11 and then I added 2 each time. Term zero will be 9.
Rule: $T = 2n + 9$

5 2, 7, 12, 17, 22, 27, …
The first term has 7 and then I added 5 each time. Term zero will be 2.
Rule: $T = 5n + 2$

6 7, 11, 15, 19, 23, 27, …
The first term has 11 and then I added 4 each time. Term zero will be 7.
Rule: $T = 4n + 7$

7 12, 15, 18, 21, 24, 27,
The first term has 15 and then I added 3 each time. Term zero will be 12.
Rule: $T = 3n + 12$

8 Rule: $T = 4n + 2$

9 Rule: $T = 2n + 12$

10 Rule: $T = 3n + 2$

Applications (pp. 70–71)

1 \$24, \$34, \$44, \$54, \$64 — $T = 10n + 14$

2 2, 3, 4, 5, 6 — $T = 1n + 1$ or $T = n + 1$

3 \$22, \$34, \$46, \$58, \$70 — $T = 12n + 10$

4 **a** \$15, \$20, \$25, \$30, \$35 — $T = 5n + 10$
b \$12, \$19, \$26, \$33, \$40 — $T = 7n + 5$
c Dodgy Dinghies, because the company is \$1 cheaper.

5 \$18, \$21, \$24, \$27, \$30 — $T = 3n + 15$

6 4, 8, 12, 16, 20 — $T = 4n + 0$ or $T = 4n$

7 \$95, \$160, \$225, \$290, \$355 — $T = 65n + 30$

8 $T = 159n + 599$

ISBN: 9780170447492

Finding a term from a rule (pp. 72–73)

1 30th term $T = 4n + 1$
$= 4 \times 30 + 1$
$= 121$

2 20th term $T = 2n + 5$
$= 2 \times 20 + 5$
$= 45$

3 40th term $T = 3n + 4$
$= 3 \times 40 + 4$
$= 124$

4 20th term $T = n + 10$
$= 20 + 10$
$= 30$

5 15th term $T = 6n + 2$
$= 6 \times 15 + 2$
$= 92$

6 10th term $T = 3n + 4$
$= 3 \times 10 + 4$
$= 34$

7 10th term $T = 4n + 8$
$= 4 \times 10 + 8$
$= 48$

8 9th term $T = 7n + 4$
$= 7 \times 9 + 4$
$= 67$

9 14th term $T = 3n + 1$
$= 3 \times 14 + 1$
$= 43$

10 18th term $T = 10n + 2$
$= 10 \times 18 + 2$
$= 182$

11 a Canoe costs $10 per hour
b $T = 10n + 5$
$= 10 \times 7 + 5$
$= \$75$

12 a Folder costs $1.99
b $T = 0.02n + 1.99$
$= 0.02 \times 40 + 1.99$
$= \$2.79$

13 a Chair costs $199.00
b $T = 749 + 199n$
$= 749 + 199 \times 8$
$= \$2341$

Finding the sequence from the rule (pp. 74–76)

1 $T = 3n + 2$

Term number (n)	1	2	3	4	5
Calculations	3 x 1 + 2				3 x 5 + 2
Value of term (V)	5	8	11	14	17

Sequence: 5, 8, 11, 14, 17

2 $T = 5n + 1$

Term number (n)	Calculations	Value of term (V)
1	5 x 1 + 1	6
2		11
3		16
4		21
5	5 x 5 + 1	26

Sequence: 6, 11, 16, 21, 26

3 $T = 2n + 6$

Term number (n)	1	2	3	4	5
Calculations	2 x 1 + 6				2 x 5 + 6
Value of term (V)	8	10	12	14	16

Sequence: 8, 10, 12, 14, 16

4 $T = 6n + 3$

Term number (n)	1	2	3	4	5
Calculations	6 x 1 + 3				6 x 5 + 3
Value of term (V)	9	15	21	27	33

Sequence: 9, 15, 21, 27, 33

5 $T = 4n + 1$

Term number (n)	1	2	3	4	5
Calculations	4 x 1 + 1				4 x 5 + 1
Value of term (V)	5	9	13	17	21

Sequence: 5, 9, 13, 17, 21

6 $T = 5n + 4$

Term number (n)	1	2	3	4	5
Calculations	5 x 1 + 4				5 x 5 + 4
Value of term (V)	9	14	19	24	29

Sequence: 9, 14, 19, 24, 29

7 $T = 7n + 10$

Term number (n)	1	2	3	4	5
Calculations	7x1+10				7x5+10
Value of term (V)	17	24	31	38	45

Sequence: 17, 24, 31, 38, 45

ISBN: 9780170447492

Cross-number (p. 77)

[1] 3	4	5	[2] 6		[3] 12	15	18	[4] 21
5			10		14			23
7		[5] 13	14	15	16	[6] 17		25
[7] 9	12	15	18		[8] 18	21	24	27
		17				25		
[9] 13	16	19	[10] 22		[11] 28	29	30	[12] 31
17		[13] 21	24	27	30	33		33
21			26		32			35
[14] 25	26	27	28		[15] 34	35	36	37

Challenge 4 (p. 78)

1

2	1	2	4	6	8	10	11	12	13
6	9	12	15	18	11	14	15	16	23
8	14	1	6	9	14	17	20	23	25
1	3	6	8	12	17	21	25	29	33
3	7	11	15	19	20	25	30	32	34
5	9	16	20	21	22	25	35	36	35
7	11	21	23	25	27	29	36	37	36
9	15	20	26	31	32	33	34	35	37
12	14	25	29	33	37	41	43	44	42
15	22	27	32	33	42	43	40	45	47

2 a 22, **25**, 28, 31, **34**, **37**, 40
b 46, **50**, **54**, 58, **62**, **66**, 70
c −13, **−7**, −1, **5**, **11**, 17
d **27**, **32**, 37, **42**, **47**, 52
e −10, **−7**, **−4**, −1, **2**, **5**

Graphs (pp. 79–88)

Plotting points (pp. 79–82)

Positive coordinates (pp. 79–81)

1 a and c

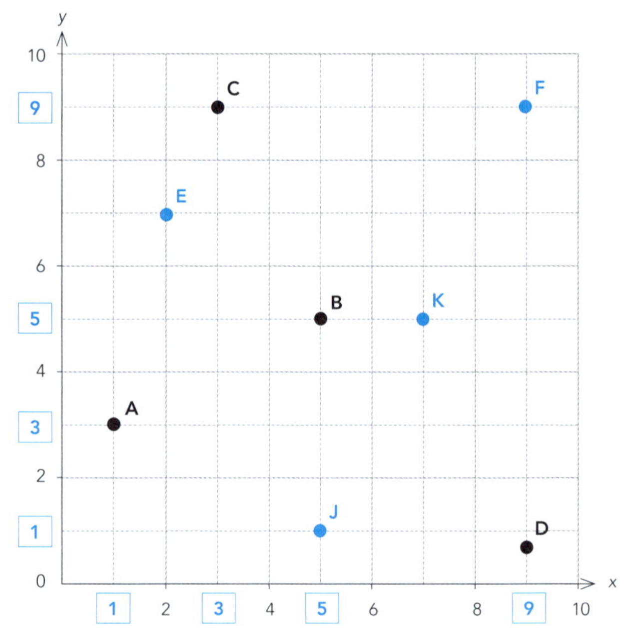

b A (1, 3) B (5, 5)
C (3, 9) D (9, 1)

2 a and c

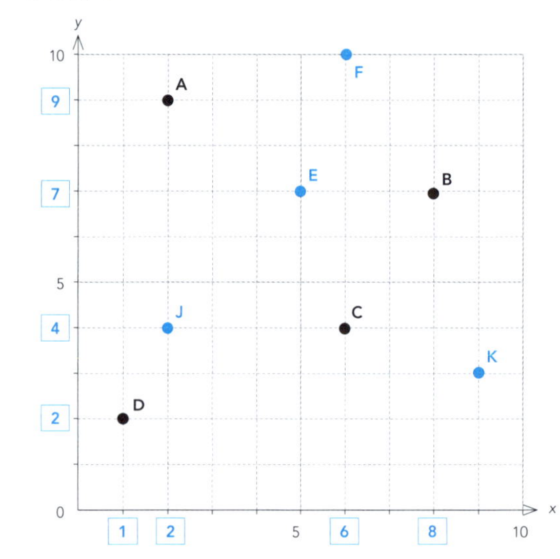

b A (2, 9) B (8, 7)
C (6, 4) D (1, 2)

Zero coordinates (p. 82)

1 A (0, 5) B (3, 0)

2

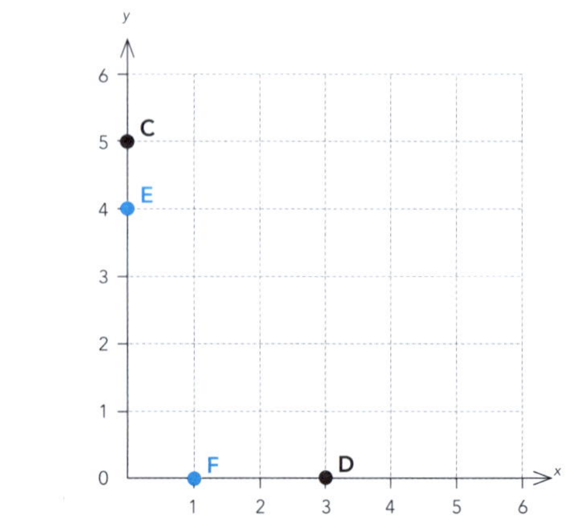

ISBN: 9780170447492

Putting it together (p. 83)

A (2, 4)
B (10, 6)
C (0, 10)
D (5, 8)
E (4, 1)
F (9, 11)
G (7, 5)
H (0, 0)

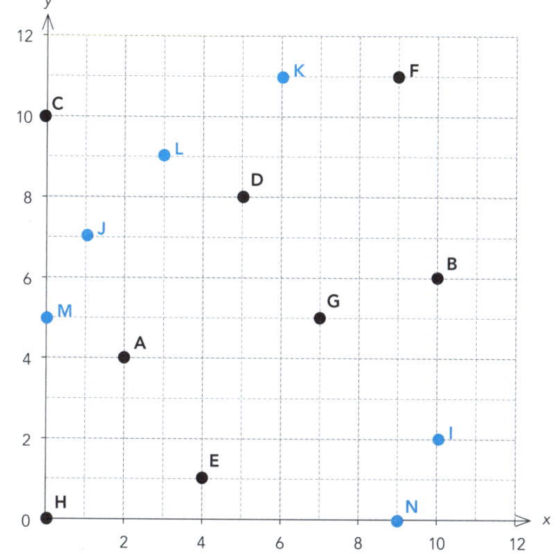

Plotting a pattern on a graph (pp. 84–88)

1

Number (n)	Value of term (V)	Coordinates
0	3	(0, 3)
1	5	(1, 5)
2	7	(2, 7)
3	9	(3, 9)
4	11	(4, 11)
5	13	(5, 13)
6	15	(6, 15)

Find the rule: V = 2 x pattern number + 3
Tidy it up: $V = 2n + 3$
Plot the points:

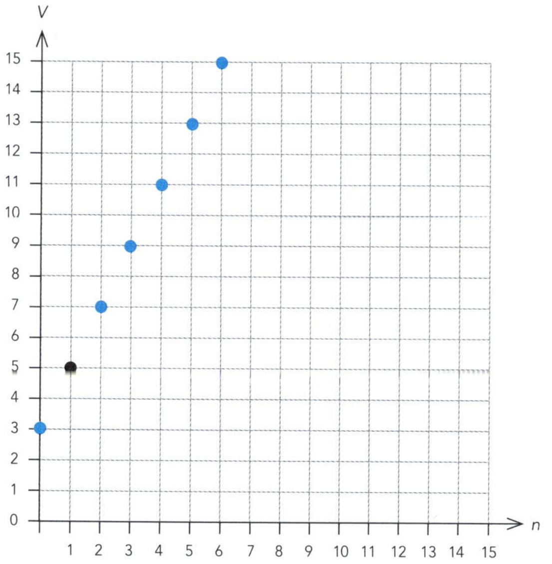

2

Number (n)	Value of term (V)	Coordinates
0	4	(0, 4)
1	5	(1, 5)
2	6	(2, 6)
3	7	(3, 7)
4	8	(4, 8)
5	9	(5, 9)
6	10	(6, 10)

Find the rule: V = 1 x pattern number + 4
Tidy it up: $V = 1n + 4$
or $V = n + 4$
Plot the points:

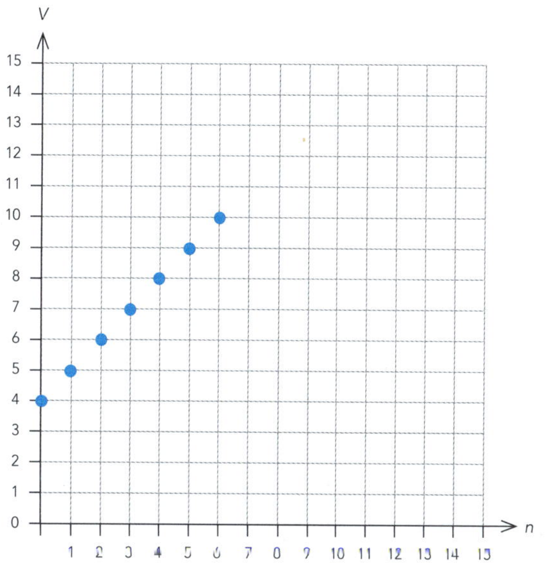

3

Number (n)	Value of term (V)	Coordinates
0	0	(0, 0)
1	4	(1, 4)
2	8	(2, 8)
3	12	(3, 12)
4	16	(4, 16)
5	20	(5, 20)
6	24	(6, 24)

Find the rule: V = 4 x pattern number + 0
Tidy it up: $V = 4n + 0$
or $V = 4n$

ISBN: 9780170447492

Plot the points:

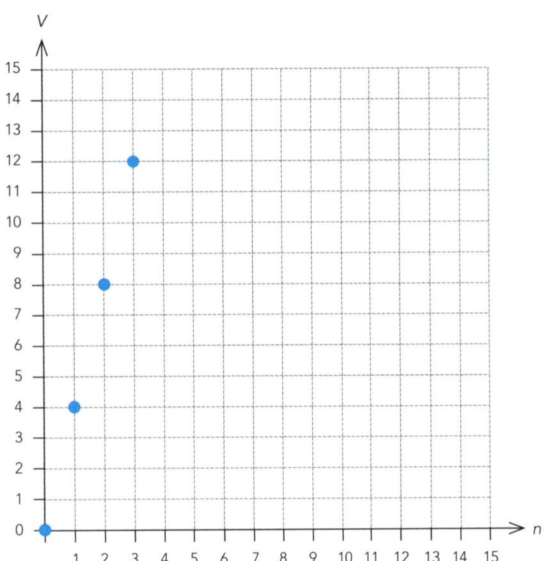

4

Number (n)	Value of term (V)	Coordinates
0	1	(0, 1)
1	4	(1, 4)
2	7	(2, 7)
3	10	(3, 10)
4	13	(4, 13)
5	16	(5, 16)
6	19	(6, 19)

Find the rule: V = 3 x pattern number + 1

Tidy it up: $V = 3n + 1$

Plot the points:

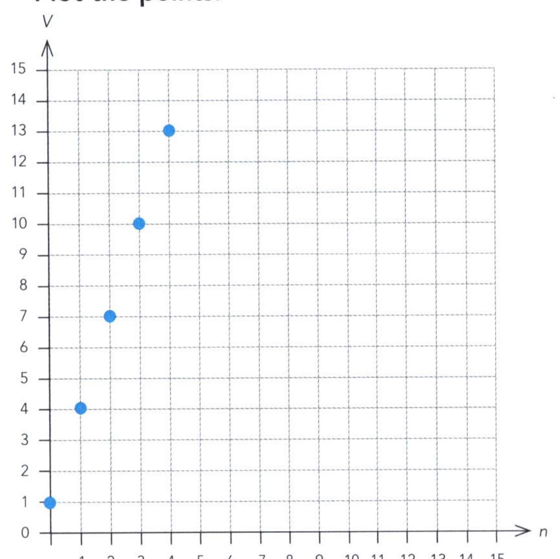

Revision 1 (pp. 89–92)

1 **a** $n - 4$ **b** $\frac{n}{4}$

2 **a** $-8p^2$ **b** 4
c $14a$ **d** $c - 5d$
e $-6m^2n$ **f** $3e$
g $2gh$ **h** $\frac{1}{3y}$

3 **a** 32 **b** 5
c 50 **d** –9

4 **a** The variables are C, which stands for **the total cost of admission plus r rides**, and r, which stands for **the number of rides**.
b They are called variables because **they can change**.
c $C = 12 + 8r$
d $C = 12 + 8r$
$= 12 + 8 \times 7$
$= \$68$

5 **a** $a = -2$ **b** $b = 48$
c $c = -5$ **d** $d = 5$
e $e = 4$ **f** $f = 18$

6 **a** $n - 5 = 20$, $n = 25$ **b** $3n = 24$, $n = 8$

7

	Question	Instruction	Answer
a	$5a - 2b - 4 + b$	Simplify	$5a - b - 4$
b	$2d^2$ if $d = -3$	Evaluate	18

8 **a**

b

Term number (n)	0	1	2	3	4	5	6
Number of popsicle sticks (P)	1	6	11	16	21	26	31

c The first term has **six** sticks and then I added **five** each time.

d Number of popsicle sticks
= **5** x term number + **1**
$P = 5n + 1$

e

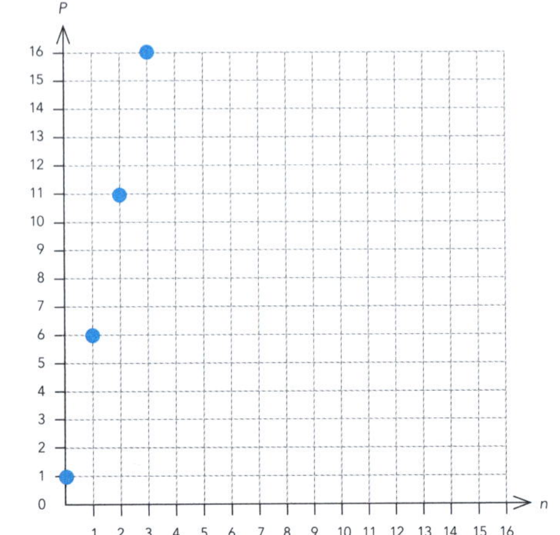

 ISBN: 9780170447492

f $P = 5 \times 50 + 1$
$= 251$

9

Term value (n)	0	1	2	3	4	5
Value of term (V)	12	16	20	24	28	30

Rule: $V = 4n + 12$

10 a $T = 6n + 13$

b The 15th term $= 6 \times 15 + 13$
$= 103$

11 $V = 3n - 10$

Term number (n)	1	2	3	4
Calculations	$3 \times 1 - 10$			$3 \times 4 - 10$
Value of term (V)	−7	−4	−1	2

The next two terms of this sequence are:
5, 8

12 a $3.49

b $T = 3.49 \times 6 + 5.99$
$= \$26.93$

13 $T = 6.99n + 15.99$

Revision 2 (pp. 93–96)

1 a $2n$ b n^2

2 a $-2p^3$ b $5b$

c $-3a$ d $\frac{4}{c}$

e 9 f $-30ab^2$

g $c - 3d + 9$ h $p^2 + p$

3 a 5 b −9

c 3 d 12

4 a The variables are C, which stands for **the total cost for a gate and p posts**, and p, which stands for **the number of posts**.

b They are called variables because **they can change**.

c $C = 70 + 14p$

d $C = 70 + 14p$
$= 70 + 14 \times 30$
$= \$490$

5 a $a = 17$ b $b = 28$

c $c = 5$ d $d = -13$

e $e = -4$ f $f = -24$

6 a $n + 6 = 13$
$n = 7$

b $\frac{n}{2} = 18$
$n = 36$

7

	Question	Instruction	Answer
a	$60 = -12a$	Solve	$a = -5$
b	$7b - b^2 + 1 - b$	Simplify	$6b - b^2 + 1$

8 a

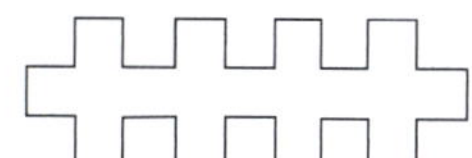

b

Term number (n)	0	1	2	3	4	5	6
Number of popsicle sticks (P)	4	12	20	28	36	44	52

c The first term has **twelve** sticks and then I added **eight** each time.

d Number of popsicle sticks
$= \mathbf{8} \times$ term number $+ \mathbf{4}$
$P = \mathbf{8n + 4}$

e

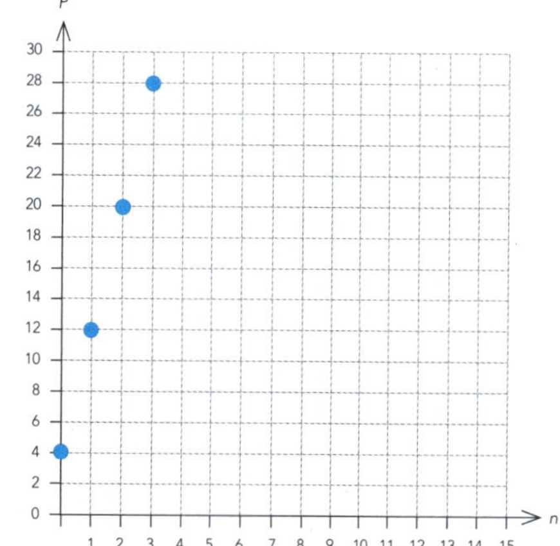

f $P = 8 \times 50 + 4$
$= 404$

9

Term value (n)	0	1	2	3	4	5
Value of term (V)	8	11	14	17	20	23

Rule: $V = 3n + 8$

10 a $T = 7n + 3$

b The 15th term $= 7 \times 25 + 3$
$= 178$

11 $V = 15n + 10$

Term number (n)	1	2	3	4
Calculations	$15 \times 1 - 100$			$15 \times 4 - 100$
Value of term (V)	25	40	55	70

The next two terms of this sequence are:
−25, −10

12 a $24.99

b $T = 6.99 \times 5 + 24.99$
$= \$59.94$

13 $T = 1.99n + 11.99$

ISBN: 9780170447492